ROADS to
FAMiLY

RACHEL HS GINOCCHIO

ROADS to

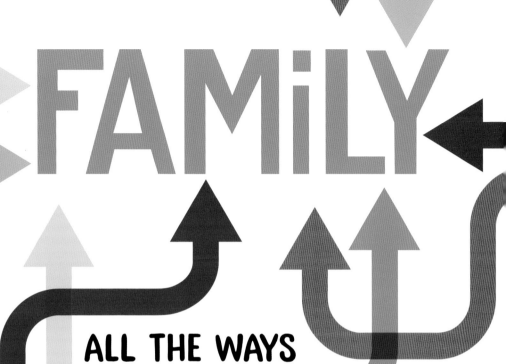

FAMILY

ALL THE WAYS

WE COME TO BE

RACHEL HS GINOCCHIO

TWENTY-FIRST CENTURY BOOKS / MINNEAPOLIS

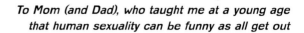

*To Mom (and Dad), who taught me at a young age
that human sexuality can be funny as all get out*

Some names have been changed to protect the privacy of interviewees.

First paperback edition published in 2024
Text copyright © 2023 by Rachel HS Ginocchio

Twenty-First Century Books™
An imprint of Lerner Publishing Group, Inc.
241 First Avenue North
Minneapolis, MN 55401 USA

For reading levels and more information, look up this title at www.lernerbooks.com.

Illustrations on pages 9, 11, 12, 13, 20, 31, 47, 49, and 50 by Mel Latthitham
Arrows design element: jirawat phueksriphan/Shutterstock.

Main body text set in Adobe Garamond Pro.
Typeface provided by Adobe Systems.

Library of Congress Cataloging-in-Publication Data

Names: Ginocchio, Rachel HS, author.
Title: Roads to family : all the ways we come to be / Rachel HS Ginocchio.
Description: Minneapolis : Twenty-First Century Books, [2023] | Includes bibliographical references and index. | Audience: Ages 11–18 | Audience: Grades 7–9 | Summary: "This informative compendium goes beyond the basics of sexual reproduction to examine the diversity of family creation. Using interviews with individuals and families, Rachel Ginocchio breaks down in vitro fertilization, surrogacy, adoption, and more"—Provided by publisher.
Identifiers: LCCN 2022023602 (print) | LCCN 2022023603 (ebook) | ISBN 9781728424545 (library binding) | ISBN 9798765643327 (paperback) | ISBN 9781728462707 (ebook)
Subjects: LCSH: Human reproduction—Juvenile literature. | Human reproductive technology—Juvenile literature.
Classification: LCC QP251.5 .G56 2023 (print) | LCC QP251.5 (ebook) | DDC 612.6—dc23/eng/20220713

LC record available at https://lccn.loc.gov/2022023602
LC ebook record available at https://lccn.loc.gov/2022023603

Manufactured in the United States of America
1-49324-49440-1/24/2024

Contents

INTRODUCTION

How to Make a Family

HAVE YOU EVER WONDERED WHERE BABIES COME from? Maybe you were a little kid when you first peppered a parent with questions. Or maybe an older sibling or classmate took it upon themselves to share their vast wealth of knowledge with you. Perhaps a grandparent read you a picture book that sparked your curiosity. If you are reading this book now, then you are probably quite a bit older than the first time you asked about human reproduction. That means you are at a great age to hear a more in-depth (and much more interesting!) answer to this question.

This book will do just that. It is filled with real-life stories from people who took a number of different routes to build their families. Though each story is unique, they all have one thing in common: advances in science and medicine were necessary to grow each family. We will explain how human reproduction works—sometimes on its own, and sometimes with help—to create a human.

ROADS TO FAMILY

You will see that human reproduction can get quite complicated. Adding children to a family involves people and their bodies, their relationships, their worries, their hopes, and their dreams. With all the nuances of the human experience, it's no surprise that growing a family can be full of emotional, biological, financial, legal, and logistical complications.

This book explains not only the science of human reproduction but also how families are defined, made, and reshaped. While we can't cover every possible scenario of how a family comes to be, we hope that you will see some element of your own experience (and those of your friends, family, and peers) in the wide variety of stories shared in this book.

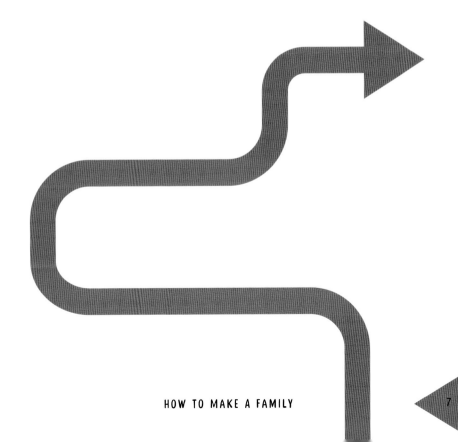

CHAPTER 1

Baby-Making Basics

YOU CAN THINK OF THE HUMAN BODY AS A SET OF transportation systems. Our digestive system brings in food, extracts nutrients, and gets rid of waste products. The circulatory system delivers nutrients and oxygen to our muscles and organs. Our nervous system carries instructions to and from our brain so that we can think, speak, and move. Our reproductive system is a series of tunnels and tubes that transport egg and sperm cells from where they are made to where they need to go to create a pregnancy.

By the time we are born, most systems in our body can do their jobs. But our reproductive system isn't fully functional until many years later, when we go through puberty. Puberty is a developmental stage that generally starts between ages eight and fourteen and lasts a few years. During puberty, most people experience significant physical, intellectual, emotional, and social changes. It's also when most people's reproductive systems become capable of creating a pregnancy.

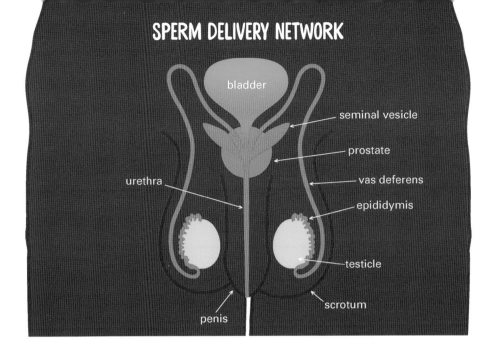

SPERM DELIVERY NETWORK

bladder
seminal vesicle
prostate
urethra
vas deferens
epididymis
testicle
penis
scrotum

The Sperm Transportation System

Once puberty begins, two oval-shaped testes start making and storing millions of sperm—roughly fifteen hundred per second. Sperm are the smallest cells in the body. They hold half the DNA, or genetic material, needed to create a baby. DNA is the instruction manual that's in nearly every cell. It tells the cell how to do its job and how to produce more cells.

Sperm develop in the testes for about two months before traveling to the epididymis—a narrow, tightly coiled tube. During their two-to-three-week journey through the epididymis, the sperm mature and develop the ability to swim. When the body is ready to send sperm on its way, the penis usually becomes erect. Erections happen when the spongy tissue of the penis purposefully fills with blood, causing it to become larger and stand stiffly away from the body. Muscular contractions propel the sperm to the vas deferens—the superhighway of the sperm transportation network. As the sperm travel through the vas deferens, the seminal vesicle and the prostate gland supply them with a grayish-white liquid that gives the sperm nutrition and energy. The combination of sperm and the fluid is called semen.

After the sperm fuel up, they are ejaculated out a small opening at the tip of the penis. Although it's only about half a teaspoon (2.5 ml) of fluid, semen usually contains forty to two hundred million sperm.

The Egg and Baby Transportation System

Unlike sperm, eggs are not generated during puberty. People are born with all the eggs they will ever have—about two million of them. Eggs are about the size of the period at the end of this sentence. They are the largest cells in the human body. Eggs contain the other half of the DNA necessary to make a human. Eggs are made and stored in two oval-shaped ovaries.

After puberty begins, the body prepares for a possible pregnancy each month. About every twenty-eight days, several eggs start maturing in one or both ovaries. The first egg to reach its full size pops out of the ovary. The release of an egg from the ovary is called ovulation. Short, fingerlike tentacles, or fimbriae, catch the egg and sweep it into the nearest fallopian tube. There is one fallopian tube on either side of the uterus. Around the time of ovulation, the uterus has a thick lining in preparation for a potential pregnancy.

Fertilization

To start a pregnancy, a sperm cell from one person has to join together with an egg cell from another person. Fertilization can happen in several ways, but let's start with an explanation of sexual intercourse, or sex for short. There are many different definitions of sex, but since we are looking at human reproduction, we will describe how penis-in-vagina sex works to create a pregnancy.

During this type of sex, two people bring their bodies close together, and they guide the erect penis into the vagina. The movement of their bodies can cause the penis to ejaculate semen directly into the vagina.

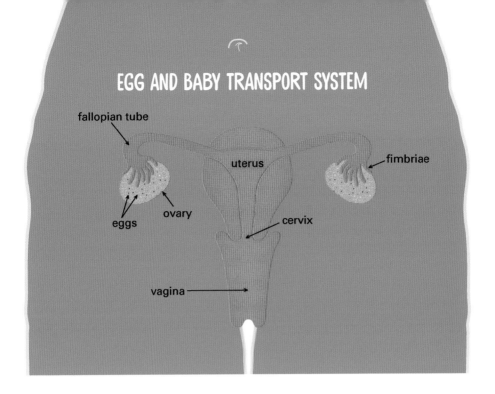

EGG AND BABY TRANSPORT SYSTEM

fallopian tube

uterus

fimbriae

ovary

eggs

cervix

vagina

Ejaculated sperm attempt to swim through the vagina, past the cervix, into the uterus, and through the fallopian tubes.

If the timing is right and an egg (or more than one egg) has just entered the fallopian tube, a sperm and an egg have twenty-four hours to try to join together. Sperm have a helmetlike structure, an acrosome, that can melt an opening in the egg's shell. After the first sperm breaks through and enters the egg, the egg's chemistry instantly changes, preventing any other sperm from getting inside. The shutout sperm die off after a few days.

THE OVULATION-MENSTRUATION CYCLE

When there is no pregnancy, the uterus sheds its thickened lining. This process is called menstruation. People ovulate and then menstruate in a monthly cycle that usually continues from puberty until menopause (which happens at about fifty years old).

MULTIPLES, PART I

Sometimes people have more than one baby at a time. These instances are called multiples—though you are likely more familiar with the terms *twins*, *triplets*, and *quadruplets*.

There are two types of multiples: fraternal and identical. Fraternal twins occur when two eggs are ovulated at the same time and are each fertilized with different sperm. Identical twins occur when one fertilized egg separates into two different embryos. Triplets, quadruplets, and other multiples can be identical, fraternal, or a mix of both.

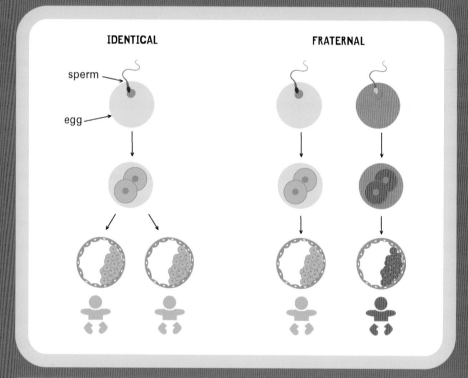

Because identical multiples develop from the same fertilized egg, they have the same DNA, or genetic material. Fraternal multiples result from separate eggs and separate sperm, so they share half their DNA, just as any other genetic siblings would.

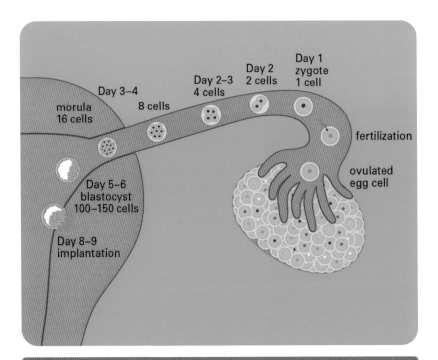

Day 1
zygote
1 cell

Day 2
2 cells

Day 2–3
4 cells

Day 3–4
8 cells

morula
16 cells

fertilization

ovulated
egg cell

Day 5–6
blastocyst
100–150 cells

Day 8–9
implantation

A fertilized egg is also known as a zygote. As the zygote moves through the fallopian tube, it divides into more cells. It becomes a morula and then a blastocyst, ready for implantation.

It takes about a day for the sperm and egg—and their DNA—to completely merge, producing the very first cell of what could grow into a new human being. After fertilization is complete, the new cell divides in half to create two cells. Then the two cells split into four cells, the four cells divide into eight cells, and so forth. The number of cells continues to double about every twelve to twenty-four hours. The bundle of cells that forms is an embryo.

The whole time that the embryo is dividing into more cells, it's traveling through the fallopian tube toward the uterus. Meanwhile, the uterine lining is becoming thicker and enriched with blood. It takes about a week for the embryo to reach the uterus. Upon arrival, the embryo is typically between 50 and 150 cells and is ready to implant, or attach. The embryo hatches out of its protective outer layer and buries into the uterine lining. The enriched lining nourishes the implanted embryo.

A DNA PRIMER

An adult human body is made of about thirty trillion cells. Cells have different jobs to do. We have brain cells, skin cells, and blood cells—just to name a few.

But how do the cells in our body know what they are supposed to do? DNA, short for deoxyribonucleic acid, is a set of instructions found in almost every cell in our body. Cells 'read' the part of the DNA code that tells them how to do their specific job.

Our DNA is wrapped tightly and precisely into packages called chromosomes. Humans usually have forty-six chromosomes. But some people have more and some people have fewer. Having a number of chromosomes other than forty-six can impact a person's health. But these differences also add to the diversity of human life.

BIO PARENT 1   **BIO PARENT 2**

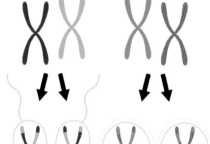

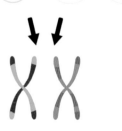

Bio Parent 1 and Bio Parent 2 each have twenty-three pairs of chromosomes. One pair from each bio parent is shown here.

To increase genetic diversity, the pair of chromosomes mix up their DNA before being placed in their own individual sex cell—either a sperm cell or an egg cell.

When an embryo forms, each bio parent contributes one of each of their chromosomes to their offspring. These form a new pair.

Gestation

Gestation is the period of time from conception until birth. Gestation usually lasts about nine months and consists of two phases: the embryonic stage and the fetal stage.

The embryonic stage of gestation encompasses the first eight weeks. During this time, the embryo's cells start to differentiate into brain, nerve, bone, muscle, and fat cells. These cells start to form tissues, tissues begin to work together as organs, and organs form systems, such as the digestive system, nervous system, and reproductive system. By the end of the embryonic stage, the very beginnings of all the essential internal and external body parts are in place.

From the ninth week on, the developing embryo is called a fetus. The fetal stage is a time of major growth and development. All the body parts and systems formed during the embryonic stage grow, grow, grow.

Birth

After growing in the uterus for about thirty-eight to forty weeks (or nine months), a baby is ready to be born. A person is almost never alone when they give birth. All over the world, spouses, partners, family, friends, doctors, nurses, physician assistants, midwives, naturopaths, coaches, doulas, and numerous other people provide medical care and support. Sometimes a person has a team to help them with their birthing experience.

Typically, labor starts with contractions. The muscular walls of the uterus tighten, then relax. As contractions continue, they cause the cervix to dilate, or open.

THE NICU

Sometimes, babies are born early and have to stay in a special section of the hospital known as the neonatal intensive care unit (NICU). There they receive medical attention until they are big enough and healthy enough to leave.

Once the cervix is fully dilated, contractions push the baby out of the uterus and through the vagina. For some people, labor takes just a few hours. For others it can take days. Enduring contractions and pushing a baby out is often intense physical and emotional work. They don't call it labor for nothing!

Another way to birth a baby is by cesarean section, or C-section. A physician administers pain medication and then makes an incision, or cut, in the abdomen and uterus. The doctor then lifts the baby out. After surgery, the doctor closes the incision.

The Right Path for Some, but Not for All

There are lots of reasons why people have sex to make babies. For many, sex is the easiest and least expensive way to grow their family. Others choose sex because their religion or culture encourages them to do so. For some, having a genetic link to their child is important, and sex is one way to accomplish this. For many, sex is the most pleasurable way to create life, and it can build intimacy between intended parents.

There are just as many reasons why sex does not work for people to grow their family. Sometimes people do not have some or all of the necessary baby-making ingredients. For example, two women may not have sperm, and a single man might need eggs and a uterus. Others may have a genetic condition they don't want to pass to offspring. Some people want children, but they do not want to have sex to bring them into their lives.

Other times, people's reproductive systems can't make a baby through sex. Infertility is a condition where people are unable to get pregnant after trying for six months to a year. A third of the time infertility involves the sperm transportation network, a third of the time something's going on with the egg transport system, and a third of the time it's both or some other reason. Sometimes a doctor knows why infertility is happening, and other times they don't.

ELECTIVE ABORTION

Approximately 15 percent of pregnancies in the United States end in an elective abortion, or pregnancy termination. This is when people choose to end a pregnancy. When people can legally end a pregnancy varies from state to state.

There are also people who are successful in creating a pregnancy through sex but the pregnancy does not progress. A miscarriage, or spontaneous abortion, is when a pregnancy ends on its own before the twentieth week of gestation—often before someone even knows they are pregnant. About 10 to 20 percent of known pregnancies end in miscarriage, and eight out of ten miscarriages happen in the first three months of gestation. Though doctors don't know all the causes of miscarriages, most are caused by problems with the embryo's genetic material.

For these and many other reasons, parents may choose another method for expanding their family. They may opt to be foster parents, adopt, or use assisted reproduction, such as insemination or in vitro fertilization.

CHAPTER 2

Insemination

INSEMINATION IS ONE TYPE OF ASSISTED REPRODUCTION.

A lot about how insemination works to create a pregnancy is the same as it is with sex. With insemination, sperm are just delivered to the egg a little differently. Unlike sex, where sperm are ejaculated directly into the vagina, with insemination, sperm are captured in a cup, vial, or other kind of container. The sperm are suctioned out of the container, usually with a syringe, and deposited into the uterus or the vagina. When sperm are placed into the uterus, it is called intrauterine insemination (IUI). When sperm are released into the vagina near the cervix, it is called intracervical insemination (ICI). People can do insemination at home or at a doctor's office.

After an insemination, the sperm do exactly what they would have done if they had been ejaculated directly into the vagina through sex. They move through the uterus to the fallopian tubes. If an egg has popped out of an ovary and into the fallopian tube when the sperm arrive, the egg and a sperm can unite. If they do, the fertilized egg divides into more cells to create an embryo, and pregnancy and birth can continue as they would have if fertilization had happened through sex.

The Necessary Elements

Insemination uses the same three components we always need to make a human—a sperm, an egg, and a uterus. But these components can come from a few different places.

Sperm Cells

Sometimes sperm for insemination comes from an intended parent—the person who intends to raise the child once they are born. But sperm can also come from a donor. A sperm donor gives their sperm to someone else so they can make a baby. For example, a single person with ovaries and a uterus might use sperm from a donor to create their family with insemination. Sperm can be used right away (fresh) or frozen and used at a later time.

Egg Cells and the Uterus

Sometimes with insemination, sperm are deposited into the body of the intended parent. So, for example, a person could be inseminated with their partner's sperm or they could be inseminated with donor sperm.

But other times, sperm are placed into the body of a genetic surrogate. A genetic surrogate carries a pregnancy and gives birth to a baby for someone else. A genetic surrogate is also called a traditional surrogate because they are the first kind of surrogate that existed. A person may use a genetic surrogate if they don't have an egg and baby transport system, are infertile, or have had multiple miscarriages. Two persons with sperm, for example, would need a genetic surrogate if they wanted to make a baby with insemination—they are missing eggs and a uterus.

In a genetic surrogacy, the surrogate's egg unites with the sperm, so it is the surrogate's DNA that joins with the genetic material of the sperm. This is why it is called genetic surrogacy—the surrogate has a genetic connection to the child.

Here is our explanation of insemination with all the people filled in:

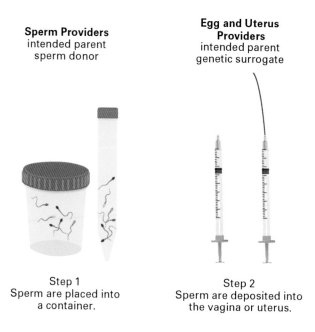

Sperm Providers
intended parent
sperm donor

Egg and Uterus Providers
intended parent
genetic surrogate

Step 1
Sperm are placed into
a container.

Step 2
Sperm are deposited into
the vagina or uterus.

You now have all the building blocks of information to understand two real-life stories from people who used insemination to create their families.

George, Elle, and David

George and his boyfriend, Finn, sat on an Australian tour bus as it bumped through town picking up other vacationers. The two men were looking forward to their trip to the tropical rain forest. But every time someone boarded the bus, Finn and George looked at each other and grimaced. Everybody who got on was so, well . . . *old*.

At the last stop, a charismatic young woman stepped onto the bus. As she made her way down the aisle, she said hello to everyone she passed. The entire bus came alive. When she sat down, Elle introduced herself to Hazel, the woman next to her, and to George and Finn, who were sitting across from her. Elle and George felt an instant connection. They spent the entire day together along with Finn and Hazel.

The next day was the last day of Elle's two-week vacation. Since George lived in Germany and she lived in the United States, she figured they'd probably never see each other again. Nevertheless, they exchanged contact information with a promise to keep in touch.

When George arrived home, he was elated to find a postcard from Elle sitting in his mailbox. George responded with an email. Elle emailed back. Soon they were regular pen pals, emailing back and forth many times over the next few months. In their communication, they opened up to each other, shared intimate details about their lives, and became close friends.

Elle's trip to Australia had been a lifelong dream vacation of hers. She had decided to go there in celebration of her fortieth birthday. She had also hoped that it would be her last big trip before becoming a mother. Elle had always wanted to be a mom, but she hadn't met anyone she wanted to have a family with. So, she had decided to do it on her own. After returning from her adventures Down Under, she got to work, researching how best to bring a child into her life.

Elle knew that she wanted to be pregnant and give birth, so the first thing on her to-do list was to determine if her reproductive system was still able to create and support a pregnancy. She went to a fertility clinic and had a thorough medical exam. The fertility doctor reported that everything was in working order.

Since Elle's body could provide the egg and uterus, insemination felt like a great option. As a single mom, however, she was missing the sperm. She would need a donor.

KNOWN, UNKNOWN, AND IDENTITY RELEASE SPERM DONORS

Those looking for a sperm donor have a few options for finding one. Some intended parents ask friends, acquaintances, or family members to be their donor. Others connect with potential donors through websites, social media, or apps. Often when people connect digitally, they chat online, video call, or meet in person to get to know one another. Regardless of how old, new, close, or distant the relationship is, if everyone involved knows one another's names and contact information, the donor is considered to be a known donor.

Other intended parents select donors from a sperm bank. These donors go through a rigorous application process, complete with interviews and questionnaires. Donors report their physical traits like hair, eye, and skin color; height and weight; race and ethnicity; religion; level of education; and interests and hobbies. They include baby photos and sometimes adult photos, voice recordings, and written responses to essay questions. They submit an extensive family medical history, noting any medical problems they or their parents, grandparents, siblings, aunts, uncles, and cousins have experienced. Donors undergo a thorough physical exam and have their blood, urine, and semen tested. Some even have genetic testing, to show that there aren't any health problems lurking in their DNA that could be passed to offspring. If everything checks out, donors are typically paid to go to the sperm bank about once

Elle mulled over her options for finding a donor and decided that her best bet was a cryobank. She started planning a sperm-donor-choosing party. She imagined her girlfriends sitting in front of the computer together, visiting sperm bank websites, and sorting through donor profiles. She knew her closest friends could help her find a healthy,

a week for a year to provide sperm samples. The samples are divided into vials of about five to twenty million sperm each and are cryopreserved, or frozen. That's why sperm banks are also called cryobanks—they store vials of frozen sperm in liquid nitrogen at −320°F (−196°C) inside big, insulated tanks. Frozen sperm can be stored and then thawed later when needed.

The cryobank creates a donor profile on their website with the information they've collected from the donor. Intended parents can sort through these profiles to find a donor that's a good fit for their family. Some intended parents look for a lot of specific traits and characteristics, and others are happy just to know that the donor and their family are healthy.

Although intended parents can learn a ton about a donor from their profile, donors from a sperm bank are considered anonymous because intended parents don't know the donor's name or contact information. Likewise, the donor has no idea how many families select their sperm or who those families are. But more and more cryobanks have an identity release program. Donors can choose to have their name and contact information released to people born from their donation when they turn eighteen.

However, it is important to keep in mind that in the digital age, being completely anonymous is not really possible. Many intended parents and donor-conceived people have discovered the identity of their donor through genetic testing, donor conception registries, and online searches. That is why anonymous donors are more commonly called unknown donors.

smart, handsome, and talented donor—one with good values and a kind personality.

Meanwhile, back in Germany, George was sorting out his own thoughts and feelings about family. George was raised in a very traditional household, with a mom, a dad, and a sister. He grew up with a blueprint

SPERM BANK CUSTOMERS

In 2000, 80 percent of people getting sperm from one of the largest sperm banks in the country were heterosexual couples. Fifteen years later, they only made up 20 percent of the customers. Half the people ordering sperm are now single women, and another 30 percent are two-woman couples.

in his mind for how his life would go: he'd meet a woman, fall in love, get married, and have two children. But by the time he was a teenager, George knew that he was gay. Since Germany did not allow same-sex couples to marry or adopt children at the time, he had to accept that he was never going to be able to get married or have a family. It took a while, but eventually he got through this tough period. He accepted himself for who he was and came out to his family and friends. It wasn't until his forties that George started thinking about kids again. But when he imagined bringing a child into the world with his boyfriend, he fretted. He didn't think that German culture was accepting of LGBTQIA+ families. He pictured his child getting teased and mocked at school for having two dads. Although he kept his dream of becoming a parent to himself, he couldn't stop thinking about it.

Then, in one of her emails to George, Elle mentioned that she had gone to a fertility clinic and was going to use donor insemination to become a mom. That got George's wheels turning. Should he offer to be Elle's sperm donor? He tossed the idea around in his mind for a couple of weeks. Finally, he got up the nerve to talk with Finn about it. "We have this amazing power to give life, which is a beautiful thing, but we obviously can't make use of it together," George explained. He paused to take stock of Finn's reaction, but he had nothing to worry about. Before George even finished speaking, Finn was on board.

But how to bring this up to Elle? She hadn't come anywhere close to asking him to be her sperm donor. They felt emotionally close and had talked regularly on the phone and communicated online, but they had only ever spent one day together back in Australia. He couldn't just send an email that said, "Hey, Elle. I just had a great hamburger for lunch. Do you want my sperm? The weather is really nice over here. OK, write again soon. Love you!"

George decided the best way was to just be simple and direct. In an email, he told Elle that she was very dear to him and that he would love to help her create life. He didn't want to make it hard for her to say no if she didn't like the idea, so he left it at that.

The email totally surprised Elle. She immediately picked up the phone and called him. She didn't care that it was two in the morning in Germany. The two talked for a long time. The more they discussed it, the more the idea of George being Elle's sperm donor felt like a real possibility.

Elle liked the idea of having a known donor. She would be aware of any worrisome mental or physical health problems that could be passed to her child. In addition, her child's genetic identity would never be a mystery. Her child would be able to ask George anything they wanted to know about him, his family, and their ancestry.

Elle talked it over with her family and friends. At first, they weren't sure about Elle's plan. They didn't think that Elle knew George well enough for him to be her donor. They didn't know how she could trust someone that she hadn't spent that much time with. What if he lied about his health? What if he wanted to be the child's father, or to play a larger role in the child's life than Elle wanted?

But Elle knew that she and George had a genuine friendship. George was honest, kind, and had a good heart. He loved his family, and they were supportive of him. He was also smart, and it didn't hurt that he was very cute. Elle had a good gut feeling about George's offer.

But before moving forward, they first needed to see if George could even be a donor. He headed to his doctor's office for a medical exam and semen analysis. In a semen analysis, doctors look at how much sperm is in the semen (quantity), how the sperm are shaped (morphology), and how well the sperm swim (motility). These factors can have a big impact on whether sperm is likely to fertilize an egg. George's semen was also tested for sexually transmitted infections (STIs). Semen can carry infectious diseases, just as other bodily fluids can. STI testing assured Elle that neither she nor any potential fetus could get a bacterial or viral infection from George's semen. George passed all the medical tests. From a health perspective, there was no reason he couldn't be a sperm donor.

George and Elle knew how consequential their decision was. If they had a child together, no matter what happened with their friendship, they would be bonded for life. If they were going to do this, they had to be willing to have a lifelong connection. They had enjoyed spending time together that one day in Australia, but who wouldn't be agreeable while vacationing in a beautiful, tropical rain forest? Could they get along in the humdrum of everyday life? They were there for each other through phone calls and email, but could they work through problems and disagreements face-to-face? Before bringing a child into the world together, they needed to answer these questions for themselves.

George hopped on an airplane bound for Texas, where Elle lived and worked as a pediatrician. They hoped that if they spent more time together, they'd know if their idea was absolutely fantastic or spectacularly bad! As George sat on the airplane, he wondered if he was doing the right thing. But he knew the answer the moment he saw Elle at the airport. As he walked toward her, George had a strong gut feeling that making a baby with Elle was the right thing to do.

During George's visit, they tackled the legal side of things. Elle had found a family attorney who was familiar with the laws around assisted reproduction and all the ins and outs of using insemination with known sperm donors. The lawyer helped George and Elle create a donor agreement.

DONOR AGREEMENTS

When donors and intended parents work with a cryobank, they sign legal agreements. Donors are never considered a parent and are not legally, financially, socially, or emotionally responsible for any children that result from their sperm. Intended parents accept all responsibility for any children born from the donated sperm. Even if a donor conceived person or their parent(s) happen to discover who the donor is (or vice versa), donors can't legally demand to be recognized as a parent or to play a role in the person's life, and intended parents cannot legally ask the donor to pay for any expenses.

When an intended parent or parents work with a known donor, they usually put together a donor agreement similar to those used at sperm banks. In it, the donor signs away their legal right to parent a child that results from their donation, and the intended parent(s) agrees to take all responsibility for raising the child. Since the donor and intended parent(s) know each other, the agreement often specifies how involved the donor will be after the baby is born. Known donor agreements can be brief or detailed, but creating one helps iron out disagreements that might come up during the pregnancy and after the birth of the baby.

From a legal standpoint, using a known donor can sometimes be a bit trickier than using an unknown donor. Usually, intended parents and known donors stick to their donor agreement. Thousands and thousands of known donor relationships go off without a hitch. But things don't always go smoothly. After the baby is born, a known donor may decide that they want to be more involved or even be considered the child's legal parent. Or an intended parent might decide that they want the donor less involved than they originally agreed to. When people have a change of heart, things can get complicated. Sometimes conflicts between intended parents and donors end up in court. A signed agreement prepared by an attorney before even attempting a pregnancy can help the judge resolve disagreements and come to a fair decision.

In addition to a donor agreement, Elle paid George five dollars in front of the attorney. This established the interaction as a business transaction much like a cryobank pays a sperm donor. The exchange of money helped make it super clear that George's role was as a donor and not as a parent.

Finalizing the legal agreement was not easy for George. He lost a couple of nights of sleep over making the decision to sign over his parental rights to Elle. By doing so, his name would not go on the baby's birth certificate. But he signed the paperwork because he knew that ultimately, it was the right thing to do for Elle, the child, and himself.

Although George would not be considered the child's father legally, they both wanted George to be part of the child's life. Elle and George had long conversations about how involved he would be. George and Elle had every intention of continuing their friendship, regardless of whether they had a baby together. But they also acknowledged that relationships often change over time. George and Elle agreed that even if they had a falling out or their friendship ended, the child would always have a right to reach out to George and ask him questions.

Elle and George also discussed what they would tell a child one day about their conception story. George joked, "Are we going to tell them that they were shaken around in a petri dish and then *bang*, you came to be?" That kind of explanation sounded simplistic, technical, and clinical. It did not match the love they felt for each other or for the child they were hoping to bring into the world. They weren't sure how they were going to explain donor insemination to their child.

"Are we going to tell them that they were shaken around in a petri dish and then *bang*, you came to be?"

George and Elle logged onto the internet hoping to find some suggestions. There they discovered something very interesting. They had planned to have the insemination done at Elle's fertility clinic, because they had assumed that's where most people did them. But they learned that many women and couples did DIY inseminations in a casual setting, like at home, at a friend's apartment, or in a hotel room. They logged off the computer knowing that they wanted to do a home insemination. It felt like a more intimate way of achieving a pregnancy—one that they could lovingly tell their child about one day. They hatched a plan.

Then it was time for George to fly back to Germany. He was armed with information on how to potentially improve his fertility. George made some lifestyle changes. Since excessive heat is bad for sperm production, he said goodbye to his tighty-whities! No more snug-fitting underwear. He switched to boxers to keep his sperm at a slightly cooler temperature. He kept his computer off his lap for the same reason. He also took vitamins and started to exercise more regularly.

Elle, too, prepared herself physically and emotionally. She took vitamins, made sure she slept well, did acupuncture, and practiced yoga. She also needed to figure out the ideal timing for the insemination. To determine the best days to try to get pregnant, Elle used something called the fertility awareness method. Fertility awareness is a way to track changes that the body goes through during its ovulation-menstruation cycle. It helps people determine when they are most fertile.

Every morning, Elle took her temperature. When a person ovulates, their body temperature goes up a little. It stays at this higher level until menstruation, usually twelve to sixteen days later. People typically take their temperature first thing in the morning and record it on a piece of paper or in an app. After tracking her temperature for a few months, Elle got a clear picture of her monthly cycle—when she'd likely ovulate and when she'd likely get her period. This was one indication as to her most fertile time.

Another clue was her cervical fluid. Throughout the month, fluid from the cervix comes out of the vagina. The color and texture changes depending on where the person is in their ovulation-menstruation cycle. When a person is most fertile, their cervical fluid is clear and wet—like egg whites. This fluid helps the sperm reach the egg.

Elle also checked the position of her cervix. The cervix prepares for a potential pregnancy each month, just like the uterus does. Most of the time the cervix is firm, sits low in the vagina, and is practically closed. As ovulation approaches, the cervix becomes soft, moves higher in the vagina, and opens up. This, along with the slick cervical fluid, enables sperm to pass through to the uterus more easily. Knowing the position of her cervix was Elle's third tip as to the right time for baby-making.

After about six months of paying attention to their fertility, George and Elle were ready to make a baby together. George and Finn flew to Texas. The minute they had grabbed their bags, Elle announced that she was pretty sure she was about to ovulate. She wanted to try an insemination as soon as they got home from the airport. But George was exhausted from the ten-hour flight. After some arguing, they agreed to wait until the morning.

The next day at Elle's house, George collected his semen in a sterile jar. He handed the sample to Elle, who took it to her bedroom. Using a plastic syringe without the needle, Elle suctioned the semen from the jar and deposited it into her vagina. The whole process took about two minutes! Afterward, Elle rested on her bed. George came in and hung out with her. The two talked and laughed. They both felt very connected to each other. "It was a really beautiful feeling," Elle remembers. As soon as she got up from resting, Elle had a hunch that the insemination had worked. Just to be sure, they did another insemination two days later.

The same night that George flew back to Germany, Elle did a home pregnancy test. This type of test detects the presence of the human chorionic gonadotropin (hCG) hormone in a urine sample. If the test shows a positive result, a person is most likely pregnant.

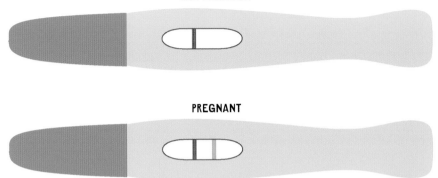

NOT PREGNANT

PREGNANT

Pregnancy tests use symbols to relate a positive or negative result. They can use plus and minus signs, smiley faces and empty circles, or other indicators depending on the brand.

When Elle saw the results, she immediately called George. Once again, she did not care that it was the middle of the night. She gave him the news—she was pregnant!

About nine months later, George came to the United States so he could be with Elle for the birth. But the due date came and went without event. Eventually, Elle's doctor recommended that they induce labor. Elle went to the hospital where her doctor gave her medication to prompt her uterus to begin contractions. But the medication didn't work. Elle ended up needing a C-section. Elle and George both felt tremendous joy the moment David was lifted from Elle's body.

Though Elle and George had talked through many potential issues with their arrangement, they were not without worries. George was absolutely certain that he would not go back on their agreement, but many times Elle worried that he would. She also wondered about George's parents. What if they thought that David should spend six months out of the year in Germany? Would they demand more from Elle and David than they were willing to give? She was completely reassured when George's parents came for a visit nine months after David's birth. It turned out that Elle had nothing to worry about. They could not have been kinder. They had no intention of getting in the way or interfering with Elle's parenting. They love David, and he calls them Oma and Opa, the German words for "grandma" and "grandpa." They send birthday presents and Christmas cards and have visited David in the United States a couple of times. David even got to go to Germany for ten days when he was three years old.

Before David arrived, George worried about Elle's large, close-knit extended family. Her mom and sisters, their husbands and kids, and some cousins spend holidays together and are very involved in one another's lives. Before he met any of them, George worried about leaving his child on the other side of the ocean with people he didn't know. But George's worries disappeared when he spent time with Elle's family. They were so warm and welcoming that he knew everything was going to be all right. Over the years, he has developed a close relationship with Elle's mom and sisters. He feels that they have welcomed him into their family.

George now lives in the United States. He remains an important person in Elle's and David's lives. They have visited one another a few times, and they sometimes text and get on FaceTime together. David knows he can reach out to George at any time. Whenever they do interact, George always tells David he loves him.

David has known his conception story since he was very young. Elle explained to him that since it takes two people to have a baby, George helped Elle make her dream of being a mom come true. David understands that although he doesn't have a dad in the same way his friends do, George loves him very much. Elle continues to answer David's questions and adds details to his story whenever he's curious.

David is now twelve. Every time he goes to a new school or joins a new sports team, kids ask about his dad. It's rare that he meets other kids that know and understand what a donor is. When he was little, he'd try to explain it, but he only kind of got it himself. It wasn't until he was about eight that he really understood enough to describe it better. "Now when people ask, I explain that a donor dad is someone who helps a mother have a baby," he says. "A lot of kids think it's strange that I don't have a mom and a dad. But I have never seen a difference in life. . . . I don't feel like it's as strange as other people think it is."

Elle is also content with her family. "Just because we are two people doesn't mean we are not complete. . . . A family can be small and still be a family."

Jake, Laura, Terra, and James

When Laura was about thirty, her ovaries stopped ovulating. This doesn't usually happen until people are older. But for Laura, it happened when she was quite young. The doctor told Laura and her boyfriend, Jake, that if they wanted to have children, they would need to adopt. But at the time, Jake and Laura weren't even thinking about starting a family. They were young, busy with work and travel, and still getting to know each other.

INFERTILITY

People faced with infertility often grapple with complex emotions. They can feel as though their bodies are betraying them since they can't do what they are biologically supposed to do—continue the human species! Men can feel like they are not "real" men. Women can feel like they are not "real" women. People in a relationship can feel as though they are not worthy as a lover or a spouse. They may even feel as though they are not worthy of being a parent. These powerful emotions of sadness, frustration, anger, anxiety, depression, and worthlessness take time to work through.

A Sperm Donor's Perspective

When Johnny and his partner John (yeah, they have the same name) were in their late twenties, they started to talk about forming a family through adoption. At the same time, Johnny received emails from two lesbian couples, both asking if Johnny was willing to be their sperm donor.

Both families wanted a queer donor. They felt that, in general, people in the queer community understood how donor conception worked. As Johnny explains, "We are all in solidarity. We get what the challenges are. We know how this could work. We know how the community is gonna roll with us."

The families also thought that Johnny would be a great fit racially and ethnically. Both couples had one white and one Black partner. Johnny made it clear that there was no way of knowing what any resulting child might look like. "I come from a multiracial Jamaican family. I obviously read as Black, but my grandma was Chinese. My dad is half Chinese, and the other half is also very multiracial—he has heritage from Lebanon and India, as well as from the African continent."

Both families, as well as Johnny and John, wanted a casual yet connected relationship after the children were born. They agreed to be honest with the kids about their conception. Johnny signed a donor agreement with each family.

The inseminations took place over six years. They were all at-home inseminations using fresh (not frozen) sperm. That meant that Johnny had to be available when the parents were ovulating. One family lived across town, so that was fairly easy. The parent that wasn't doing the insemination would drive to Johnny's house to pick up the sample. But the other couple lived in a different part of the country. Sometimes they flew to Johnny to do an insemination, sometimes he flew to them, and sometimes they met in the middle. In the midst of all the inseminations, John and Johnny adopted two children to grow their own family.

The kids now range in age from eight to twelve. The families have remained in one another's lives and enjoy vacationing together. Though the children's relatedness to one another is super clear now, it did take them a bit of time to work it all out. Johnny has fond memories of when the oldest kids were about six or seven. Though they all knew their conception story, it was then that everything started to click into place. He remembers various moments when he heard them start to figure it out. "Wait. Which one is my biological dad? Is it Uncle Johnny or Uncle John?" "Which one of you is my half-sister?" "I have a half-brother that lives across the country, right?"

So far, the kids haven't had any big questions for Johnny, but he imagines that changing when they are teenagers and start thinking more independently. He looks forward to when they might want to video chat or text and get to know him and his extended family more. For now, the kids are happy just to see their fun Uncle Johnny.

Years passed. Laura and Jake got married, and they decided they were ready for kids. While they had known about Laura's infertility for a long time, they still had to work through their tangled thoughts and feelings about what that meant for their family. Laura knew she had to come to terms with the fact that she would not be pregnant or birth a baby, something she had wanted since she was young. She and Jake also had to accept that they would not be creating genetic offspring together, so they would not have a genetic connection to their child. But they both knew that having a child in their family was what mattered most to them—not the route they took to get there.

They found an adoption agency close to home and began the adoption process with gusto. But in the midst of filling out forms and attending required parenting classes, Jake and Laura discovered something upsetting. The Catholic adoption agency they were working with would not allow members of the LGBTQIA+ community to adopt children through their organization. Laura and Jake were conflicted. They wanted a baby very badly, but they did not want to support an organization that they felt promoted unethical adoption practices. They didn't know what to do.

Jake's sister, Terra, felt their pain. They were close friends, so she knew what they were going through. She was there for Laura and Jake when they had to come to terms with infertility, and now she saw their anguish over the adoption agency's policy. An idea popped into her head. What if she became a surrogate for Laura and Jake? In other words, what if she was pregnant and gave birth to a baby for Jake and Laura?

Terra knew she didn't want to be a mother, but as a teen she had liked the idea of being a surrogate. But in her early twenties, Terra talked herself out of surrogacy for two main reasons: First, she did not like the idea of taking a whole bunch of fertility medication. Second and more important, she did not want to get pregnant and then learn something awful about the intended parents. What if it turned out that the husband was abusive to the wife, or something just as horrible? She knew she would not be able to relinquish a baby into a dangerous environment. What would happen to the baby?

But Jake and Laura's situation was different. She saw how much they loved each other and knew they would be amazing parents. So, on Laura's thirty-ninth birthday, Terra sent Laura and Jake a letter. In it, Terra asked if they would be open to having a conversation about her being pregnant and giving birth to their baby for them.

A week went by with no reply from Jake or Laura. Terra figured that the silence meant that they thought it was too weird. Just when Terra had given up on the idea, Jake called. He explained that although he and Laura had initially dismissed the idea, her suggestion was starting to take hold. The three adults went out to dinner and talked it over. Though they were all very good friends, this was not like any conversation they had ever had before. Every sentence started with "If we do this . . ." The

GENETIC SURROGATES

Intended parents find genetic surrogates in much the same ways that they find sperm donors. They may ask someone they know, such as a friend, acquaintance, or relative, or search for a surrogate online. Or they may use a surrogacy agency that matches intended parents and surrogates and guides them through the process.

When someone wants to be a genetic surrogate through an agency, they have to go through an extensive application. They must be healthy, be between twenty-one and thirty-two years old, and have had at least one uncomplicated pregnancy and delivery. Then they have to fill out forms and questionnaires, complete an in-depth interview, pass a criminal background check, and undergo a home inspection to prove that they live in a safe, stable environment. A doctor reviews their medical records, and they undergo an extensive mental health evaluation. Only then are they eligible to match with intended parents.

more they shared their worries and their hopes, the more they realized that surrogacy was the right path for them.

All three adults agreed that they would tell any future child the truth about their conception. As Terra explained, "We were not going to keep it a secret and then reveal it on the kid's eighteenth birthday, or anything like that." From the moment the child could ask questions and understand, the adults would be open and honest. They wanted the child to be proud of how they came into the world.

But there were some details to sort out. If Terra was their genetic surrogate, her egg would create the pregnancy. Therefore, they couldn't use Jake's sperm. If people providing the egg and sperm are closely genetically related (in this case, brother and sister), it can cause health problems for the child. They would need to use sperm from a donor. Since Jake and Laura had already accepted that they would not have a genetic link to their child when they pursued adoption, using donor sperm wasn't an issue for them. Besides, having his sister as their surrogate would actually give Jake a genetic connection to the child. As a bonus, people often thought that Laura and Terra were sisters. They both have dark hair, similar skin color, and wear glasses. They are also smart, compassionate, thoughtful, and have a warm sense of humor. So, although Laura's DNA would not be passed to the baby, the child would hopefully inherit some of the traits that she and Terra shared. Characteristically speaking, the child could be a lot like both Laura and Jake, even though neither their egg nor sperm would create the pregnancy. All three adults felt good about their decision. Better than good—they felt ecstatic!

To begin their baby-making adventure, the team made an appointment at the only nearby fertility clinic with a surrogacy program. They met with a fertility doctor to discuss their plan. The doctor did not like the idea of Terra being a surrogate. The doctor thought that once she was pregnant, Terra would get attached and refuse to hand the baby over to Jake and Laura.

The doctor preferred to work with surrogates who were already parenting their own child because he believed they were less likely to go back on a surrogacy agreement. Terra disagreed with this reasoning. To her, surrogates with their own kids obviously had a maternal instinct. They *did* get attached during pregnancy and *did* want to be a parent. To her, they were *more* likely to want to keep the baby. Terra thought that someone who knew they never wanted to be a parent was better qualified to be a surrogate.

Terra knew she wouldn't change her mind. It was annoying to have someone else tell her that they didn't believe her. To prove that she knew exactly what she was doing, Terra agreed to a mental health exam. It consisted of a psychological evaluation and a counseling session. The counselor wanted to be sure that Terra understood what was involved in surrogacy, that she was up for the challenges that might occur, that she had friends and family to provide support, and that she had no intention of parenting the child once it was born.

Terra passed the mental health screening with flying colors. The counselor's professional opinion was that the family would have a successful surrogacy arrangement. But when they reviewed the results from Terra's evaluation with the fertility doctor, he was still not convinced. He insisted that Jake and Laura also meet with the counselor. Exasperated, Terra stood up and walked out of his office. Jake and Laura followed after her.

They were really frustrated. People get pregnant all the time, and nobody questions their mental health, their knowledge about the risks and rewards of pregnancy, their ability to cope with stress, their support networks, or why they want a baby. Laura, Jake, and Terra talked all the time, and they already knew the answers to these questions.

So Laura and Jake turned to the internet to find alternatives to working with the fertility clinic. There they discovered that they could create their family the way they wanted to on their own. They found a cryobank that shipped directly to people's homes, sorted through the donor profiles on the sperm bank's website, and found a donor they liked. He had physical traits that matched their family and personality characteristics that they hoped their child would inherit. He and his extended family were healthy, and he seemed like a decent human being. They also liked that the donor was identity release.

Satisfied with their selection, Laura and Jake clicked the purchase button. A few days later, when Terra came home from work, there was a big package on her porch. She instantly knew what it was. Sure enough, inside the cardboard box was a tank of liquid nitrogen containing a vial of frozen sperm.

Over the past several months, Terra had been charting her ovulation-menstruation cycle. She checked her body temperature every day and marked it in a notebook she kept by the side of her bed. By the time the sperm arrived, she had a good idea of when her most fertile days were.

When the timing looked good, Laura went over to Terra's apartment to help her with the insemination. They read the instructions several times and followed each step carefully. After opening the tank's lid, Laura put on oven mitts to protect her hands from the dangerously cold liquid nitrogen. She carefully lifted out the rack that held the plastic vial of sperm. The vial was tiny—about half the size of her pinkie. Terra and Laura laughed at how small it was compared to the size of the tank it was shipped in.

Laura removed the vial from the rack and put it on a plate on the dresser to let it thaw. After about ten minutes, when the vial was safe to hold, Laura placed it between the palms of her hands and rolled it back and forth to warm it up. Terra and Laura gave the sperm some encouragement: "Wake up little guys. We have a job to do!"

When the sperm were warmed to body temperature, Terra took the vial into her bedroom. She used a tube with a bulb at the end called a pipette to suction the sperm out of the vial. She placed the pipette into her vagina and released the sperm. That was that!

They sent the empty tank back to the sperm bank and waited. About two weeks after the insemination, Terra took a home pregnancy test. It was negative.

They were disappointed but still determined. Laura and Jake went back online to order another sperm sample. They tried a different donor this time. When the tank arrived, Terra knew exactly how to handle the thawing and insemination all on her own. But about two weeks later, she had another negative pregnancy test.

Terra knew she didn't want to keep doing inseminations over and over. It was expensive to keep purchasing sperm, and she did not want Jake and Laura to waste their money. Perhaps Terra couldn't get pregnant. The three adults decided that the next try would be their last.

This round, Jake and Laura ordered sperm from the original donor. Terra was a pro at this point and once again did the insemination herself. But about a week later, she started to feel cramps. She told Laura that she was about to get her period. She told her brother and sister-in-law she was sorry that the insemination hadn't worked.

But Laura thought that the cramps were a sign that the insemination *had* worked. About a week later, when Terra still hadn't gotten her period, she did a home pregnancy test. Terra called Laura and Jake to tell them that she was, in fact, pregnant. It had been three months and three tries. Three times really is the charm! Laura loves to joke that "Terra knocked herself up!"

Terra had agreed to be a surrogate for the experience and out of love for her brother and sister-in-law. Not for the money. But money is a part of everyday life, and having a baby is expensive. It's rare for a surrogate's health insurance to cover their medical expenses. Instead, the intended parent(s) usually buys specific medical insurance for a surrogate. Jake and Laura were lucky. Terra's health insurance did pay for most of her medical care. Jake and Laura paid for anything that wasn't covered.

"Terra knocked herself up!"

Jake and Laura also provided Terra with a monthly stipend, a set amount of money each month so she could buy things she needed, like maternity clothes. Jake and Laura found other ways to help Terra with her living expenses. While Terra was pregnant, she bought her first house. Jake and Laura purchased a washer and dryer for her so she wouldn't have to lug her laundry to a laundromat. They also helped her upgrade her old, run-down car to one that was newer and safer.

Laura went with Terra to almost every doctor's appointment, and Jake joined them for big milestones, "like the appointment when the baby was the size of a peanut, but you could hear the heartbeat and see the head, feet, and little fingers," Terra remembers.

Laura and Jake never worried about what Terra was eating, drinking, or doing during the pregnancy. Terra lived a healthy lifestyle, and they knew she was taking good care of herself and the baby.

Throughout the pregnancy, Terra never regarded herself as the baby's mother. She knew she was carrying Jake and Laura's child. Terra guesses that if she had a child growing inside of her that she had intended to parent, she likely would have felt differently. But since that was not so, she never felt as if the baby was hers. She was not very emotional about it. Instead, she loved the experience from a scientific and medical standpoint. She was fascinated by all the amazing biology that was going on inside of her. "I was the biological vessel that could make this happen. I was the oven."

She also got a kick out of messing with people! She enjoyed telling people that she was carrying her brother's child and seeing their horrified reactions. Then she would let them in on the joke by explaining sperm donors, insemination, and genetic surrogacy.

Other than some minor aches and pains, the pregnancy went smoothly—until Terra was close to her due date. She developed high blood pressure, which could put her liver and kidneys in danger or lead to a stroke. High blood pressure can also cause complications for the baby. The baby may not get enough blood, oxygen, and nutrients.

Terra tried everything her doctor suggested, but her blood pressure refused to drop. The doctor instructed Terra to grab her overnight bag and check into the hospital. They needed to induce labor to speed things along.

At the hospital, Terra was given medication to start labor. But after many hours of long, painful contractions, her cervix was still not dilated enough for her to start pushing the baby out. The anesthesiologist gave Terra an epidural to help her with the excruciating pain. This medication numbed her body from her belly button to her upper thigh, giving her some much-needed relief.

As Terra's doctor began her shift in the wee hours of the morning, the nurses informed her that they were concerned about Terra and the baby's vitals. The doctor came into Terra's room, took one look at the monitors, and declared, "We're going to the operating room right now." Just like in the movies, the medical staff quickly raised the railings on the sides of Terra's bed, released the bed brakes, and whisked her into the operating room. Terra had an emergency C-section at 1:14 in the morning after forty-eight hours of exhausting labor.

Soon after James was born, the adults worked with their lawyer to complete some final paperwork. Many months ago, when they first began their surrogacy journey, they had put a surrogacy agreement in place. In the agreement, the adults specified that Terra intended to give birth to a child that Jake and Laura would raise. But now that James was born, Laura and Jake had to formally adopt James from Terra. Once the adoption paperwork was completed, Jake and Laura became his legal parents.

True to their original plans, James has always known his conception story. It first came up when his cousin on his mom's side, Ryan, was born with a hand that was not fully formed. Two-year-old James commented to Laura, "Mommy, I came out of your tummy with two hands, but Ry Ry only came out with one hand."

Laura explained, "Gosh, Mommy's tummy doesn't work like that.

You came out of Auntie Terra's tummy." Laura remembers that it was such a natural way to introduce James's conception story to him. From then on, whenever James had a question, all he had to do was ask.

When James was around twelve, Laura showed him the small plastic vial that the donor's sperm had come in and asked if he wanted to take a selfie with his dad. It was just a joke, of course, because the family has never considered the sperm donor to be James's dad. James reserves the name Dad for Jake. He refers to the sperm donor as "the donor."

In the fifteen-page profile they have on the sperm donor is a letter the donor wrote to his future offspring—any kids born from his sperm. In it, he wrote about life and karma, and he wished his offspring a happy life. He also offered to meet any offspring that were interested once they turned eighteen. For now, James has no interest in meeting the donor.

Even though Terra sometimes describes herself as James's bio mom, she thinks of herself as James's aunt. Terra thinks that James is a pretty remarkable human being. But all her nieces and nephews are special to her. She doesn't feel closer to James than she does to the others. Her connections to them have more to do with her relationships with them and less to do with genetics. To Terra, spending time with them, talking on the phone, eating dinners together, and sharing special occasions is what creates the closeness, not the DNA. "Biology does not a parent make," Terra notes. "It can, but at the end of the day, it doesn't really matter. Laura is one of the most loving mothers I have ever known. James is not biologically related to her, and it makes not a bit of difference."

"Biology does not a parent make . . . at the end of the day, it doesn't really matter."

James, too, thinks of Terra as his aunt, not as his mom. He uses the term *bio mom* when he's explaining things to other people, but to him, Laura is his mom, no question about it. But that didn't stop him from trying on some labels once. When James was about four, he got very mad at Laura and exclaimed, "I am going to go live with my real mom." Laura didn't let her hurt feelings show. Since she had taught middle school for many years, she knew all too well that people of all ages sometimes say hurtful things when they are angry—things they don't really mean. As Laura calmly helped James pack his suitcase so he could go live with Terra, they discussed all the things he would not be able to do at Terra's house. Terra was wonderful and an amazing aunt, but she didn't have video games and a trampoline. So, James reconsidered his decision and decided to stay home.

When asked what she'd like people to know about surrogacy, Terra explains, "If you are a woman, and you know you do not want to be a mother, you are not broken. Society tells us this, but it is not true. I hope that girls and women know that if they do not want to be a parent, that there is nothing wrong with them." She continues, "If people want the experience of being pregnant and giving birth, being a surrogate is a great option. It was a fantastic experience for me." She pauses thoughtfully and adds, "It was a fantastic experience for all of us."

As a young kid, James often found himself having to explain sperm donors, insemination, and surrogacy to other kids. They never really got it. He thinks that if a fuller explanation of human reproduction were taught in school, then he wouldn't have had to explain it. Now that he is fifteen, his friends get it, and they love to joke around about it. Sometimes when James gets a good grade, his friends tease him and say that it's because he was genetically engineered in a lab. James knows they know the truth—that he was made with an egg, sperm, and uterus, just like every human being—so he just shakes his head and laughs.

CHAPTER 3

In Vitro Fertilization

IN VITRO FERTILIZATION (IVF) IS ANOTHER FORM OF assisted reproduction. IVF differs from sex and insemination in that fertilization happens outside of the body in a medical laboratory. With IVF, mature eggs are surgically removed from the ovaries and placed in a flat, shallow container called a petri dish. Sperm are usually ejaculated into a container, just like with insemination. But some adults don't produce much sperm, and others can't ejaculate, so sperm can be surgically removed from the testes or the epididymis.

Fertilization happens in one of two ways. In one method, an embryologist adds fifty to one hundred thousand sperm to the petri dish with the eggs. The sperm swim around looking for an egg to fertilize. It is common for multiple eggs to be fertilized in the same dish. In the other method, an embryologist uses a high-powered microscope to select a single sperm and inject it directly into an egg. The embryologist does this for each of the eggs in the dish. This is called intracytoplasmic

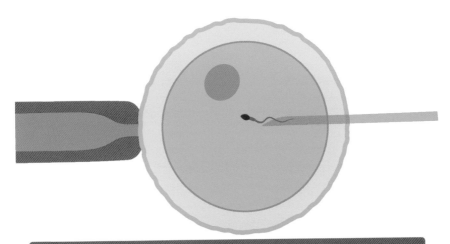

With ICSI, an embryologist gently holds an egg in place with a small pipette and uses a thin, glass needle to inject a single sperm into it. ICSI can increase the chance of—but does not guarantee—fertilization.

sperm injection (ICSI). ICSI is the most common way to fertilize eggs during IVF.

Once an egg and sperm cell join together, the fertilized egg starts to divide into more cells to create an embryo, just as it does when fertilization happens inside the body from sex or insemination.

After the embryos develop in the petri dish for three to six days, a fertility doctor transfers one or more of the embryos to the uterus. If an embryo attaches to the uterus, gestation and birth can continue as usual.

The Necessary Elements

IVF can seem complicated, but IVF uses the same three parts we always need to form a little one—sperm, egg, and uterus. They just come along on different roads.

Sperm Cells

Since the sperm is outside of the body in a container, it can come from the intended parent or from a sperm donor.

Egg Cells

Since eggs are also removed from the body and collected in a container for IVF, they too can come from an intended parent or from an egg donor. An egg donor gives their eggs to someone else so they can grow their family. Just like sperm, eggs can also be cryopreserved, or frozen.

The Uterus

Since embryos are created in a petri dish, we can do the same things with them as we do with egg and sperm cells that are outside of the body. Embryos can be used right away or frozen. They can be donated to another family, placed in the uterus of the intended parent, or transferred to the uterus of a gestational surrogate.

A gestational surrogate is pregnant with and gives birth to a baby for someone else. Unlike a genetic surrogate, the gestational surrogate's eggs are not used to create the pregnancy. With IVF, the eggs come from the intended parent or from a donor. So the gestational surrogate's genetic material is not passed to the child. The DNA comes from the

IVF WINS THE NOBEL PRIZE

Louise Brown was born on July 25, 1978. She was the world's first baby born from IVF. At the time, her birth rocked the world, and the scientist who pioneered the procedure won the Nobel Prize in Physiology or Medicine. As an adult, Brown talks about how proud she is of her personal role in the advancement of medical science. About forty years after Louise's birth, it is estimated that at least eight million babies across the world have been born from IVF. Almost 2 percent of all births in the US are the result of IVF, 2 to 7 percent of all the births in Europe, and 7 percent of all births in Japan.

intended parent or the egg donor—whoever provided the egg. Although most families use the term *surrogate* for both types of surrogates, there is a big distinction! Most people who work in the fertility industry prefer to use two distinct terms: *genetic surrogate* and *gestational carrier*.

Here is our explanation of IVF, with all the different people who can play a role in the process:

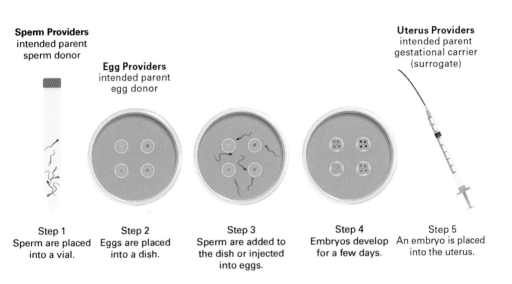

Sperm Providers
intended parent
sperm donor

Egg Providers
intended parent
egg donor

Uterus Providers
intended parent
gestational carrier
(surrogate)

Step 1
Sperm are placed into a vial.

Step 2
Eggs are placed into a dish.

Step 3
Sperm are added to the dish or injected into eggs.

Step 4
Embryos develop for a few days.

Step 5
An embryo is placed into the uterus.

Steve, Stephanie, Nate, Lizzie, Haley, Lily, and Rob

The first time they met, Steve and Stephanie hit it off. They started out as friends, began dating, fell in love, and then tied the knot. Soon after, they began talking about growing their family. Though Steve had three kids from a previous marriage whom Stephanie adored, Steve and Stephanie also wanted kids together. The tricky part was that Steve had had a vasectomy.

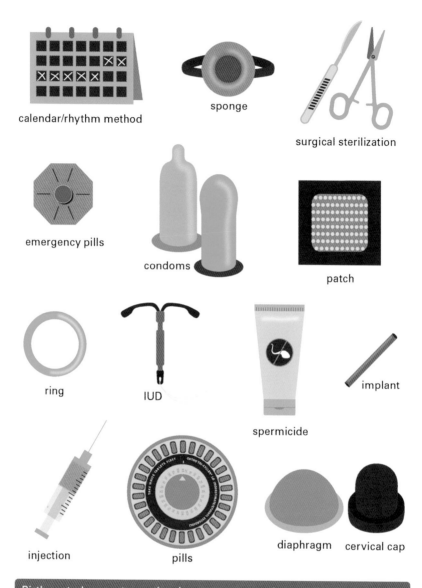

calendar/rhythm method

sponge

surgical sterilization

emergency pills

condoms

patch

ring

IUD

spermicide

implant

injection

pills

diaphragm

cervical cap

Birth control, or contraception, is a common way that people prevent pregnancy. There are lots of different birth control options to meet the varying needs of individuals. Some methods, such as the pill or shot, use hormones to pause the ovulation-menstruation cycle. Others, like condoms and diaphragms, create a barrier so the egg and sperm can't meet. Condoms also protect against sexually transmitted infections. Surgical sterilization is a permanent way to prevent pregnancy. Talking to a health-care provider about birth control can help someone find the option that's right for them.

People who want to have sex without getting pregnant can use birth control. Hormonal pills and condoms are two common forms of birth control. A vasectomy is another kind. A surgeon cuts or seals off the vas deferens in the reproductive system so that after leaving the epididymis, the sperm hit a dead end. Someone can still ejaculate semen, but the semen does not have any sperm in it. A vasectomy is meant to be a permanent way to prevent a pregnancy. But sometimes people change their minds. In these instances, a doctor can try to reattach the tubes that have been cut or sealed. Sometimes a vasectomy reversal works, and sometimes it doesn't.

Steve and Stephanie decided to tell the children their plans. On Father's Day, the whole family gathered around the dinner table. Nate (eighteen years old), Lizzie (fifteen), and Haley (seven) listened as their dad announced that he was going to reverse his vasectomy so that they could add another kid to the family. Nate stared at his dad wide-eyed. He tilted his head toward Stephanie and asked, "What? Do you want my father to die?"

Stephanie didn't know why he would ask such a thing. Neither a vasectomy nor a vasectomy reversal is major surgery. But Steve knew exactly why Nate had asked. Seven years ago, while he was recovering at home after his vasectomy, Steve had passed out. Low levels of potassium in Steve's bloodstream, combined with the pain medication he took for the surgery, had caused his heart to stop. His wife found him unconscious on the bathroom floor and immediately called 911. The EMTs got there in time to revive him. Though Steve's cardiac arrest had nothing to do with the vasectomy itself, in Nate's mind there was a direct link between the vasectomy and his dad nearly dying. He was convinced that reversing the vasectomy was going to cause his dad's heart to stop again.

Steve and Stephanie convinced the kids that Steve's heart would be fine. Steve went ahead with the surgery to repair his tubes. A few months later, Stephanie and Steve were ready to start making a baby together.

To increase the likelihood of success, Stephanie tracked her periods, temperature, and cervical fluid. In addition to these fertility awareness methods, about ten days after her period started, Stephanie began using an ovulation predictor kit. These work like home pregnancy tests, in that they detect a specific hormone in the urine. When the ovulation predictor kit shows a positive result, ovulation is likely to happen within thirty-six hours.

Stephanie had to test her urine around the same time every day to get an accurate result. So it wasn't always convenient to use an ovulation predictor kit. She remembers having to pee on the test strip at a friend's house, at work, in a public restroom, and in a porta potty. If she or Steve were in a crowded place where they could not openly discuss the results—like at a ball field or at work—Stephanie would text Steve a picture of the test results.

Month after month, Stephanie used fertility awareness and ovulation predictor kits. Month after month, Steve and Stephanie tried to conceive. Month after month, they were unsuccessful.

Steve and Stephanie assumed that they weren't getting pregnant because Steve's vasectomy reversal hadn't worked. They figured he was "shooting blanks"—that his semen still had no sperm. They went to a fertility doctor to find out. But when the doctor did a semen analysis and medical exam on Steve, everything looked fine. The tubes had reattached successfully, and the sperm had a clear path. The quantity, mobility, and morphology of the sperm all looked normal.

So, the doctor examined Stephanie. He checked her hormone levels to estimate the number and quality of eggs in her ovaries and did an ultrasound to see how her uterus looked. An ultrasound uses sound waves to display the inside of the body onto a screen. The ultrasound revealed that Stephanie had a polyp in her uterus. A polyp is a growth that can be as small as a sesame seed or as large as a golf ball. Polyps aren't usually cancerous, but when they grow in the uterus, they can make it hard to get pregnant. Stephanie had surgery to remove the polyp.

After the surgery, Stephanie took fertility medication to help with ovulation. Fertility medication is made of hormones that stimulate the ovaries to do what they normally do but more so. Sometimes, instead of one egg popping out of the ovary and into the fallopian tube, two or three eggs are ovulated. The hope is that with more eggs in the fallopian tube, the higher the chance of fertilization and the better the odds of a pregnancy. But the fertility medication did not help. Steve and Stephanie kept trying, but Stephanie did not get pregnant.

It was time for Steve and Stephanie to start thinking about assisted reproduction: insemination and IVF. Their doctor recommended they start with IUI. Though Steve's sperm looked healthy, getting them closer to the egg meant they had less swimming to do. Perhaps this would give them a better chance of fertilizing Stephanie's eggs. If IUI didn't work after three tries, they'd likely need to consider using IVF.

This was some heavy stuff to take in. Stephanie and Steve knew that not everyone has the privilege of creating life without assistance, but they wanted that to be their child's story. They wondered about IUI and IVF. If fertilization happens in a lab, is the child still created out of love? After talking about it and sharing their feelings, Stephanie and Steve came to see that assisted reproduction is still an act of love, albeit a less conventional one than "making love" to have a baby.

> If fertilization happens in a lab, is the child still created out of love?

As they were navigating their feelings about creating life in a lab, something happened that really helped them move forward. One day at church, they saw their fertility doctor sitting just a few pews in front of them. They were relieved to see him there. This opened the door to additional conversations with him, which enabled Stephanie and Steve to come to terms with their decision about using assisted reproduction. They tried three IUIs. Each time, Stephanie had to chart her ovulation-menstruation cycle, go into her fertility clinic for blood tests and ultrasounds and, when the timing was right, return for the insemination. Steve, too, had to go to the fertility clinic each time to provide the semen. After Steve made his deposit into a sterile medicine cup, the embryologist prepared the sperm, then passed it to the fertility doctor, who did the insemination.

The IUIs were inconvenient and expensive, and doing them month after month was emotionally challenging. With each insemination, they'd get excited for a possible pregnancy, and then two weeks later, their hopes would be dashed by a negative pregnancy test.

After three unsuccessful IUIs, their fertility doctor did another ultrasound to see what was going on. No other polyps had developed, but the doctor found that Stephanie had endometriosis—where tissue that typically grows inside the uterus grows outside of it. The tissue blocked Stephanie's fallopian tubes and prevented the eggs and sperm from meeting. It was also quite painful. Stephanie had surgery to clear the endometriosis from her tubes. But a few months later, the endometriosis returned and another polyp developed. Once again, the surgeon successfully extracted the polyp. However, the endometriosis was so bad that he had to remove one of Stephanie's fallopian tubes.

Stephanie was devastated. Even though she was doing everything she could, she couldn't help thinking, What's wrong with me? She had lots of siblings, and nobody else had problems getting pregnant. She didn't know why her body wasn't working the way it was "supposed" to.

If they wanted a baby, the next step was IVF. Steve and Stephanie knew they might need extra emotional support, so they shared their plans with their family. They explained that IVF does not always work the first time or the second time or the third time or ever. They told them that Stephanie had to take a large quantity of hormones that might leave her feeling bloated, nauseated, anxious, or depressed. Stephanie and Steve wanted their family to know that they might be headed for more rough times.

FRIENDLY BUT NOT-SO-HELPFUL ADVICE

When people have difficulty getting pregnant, friends, family, and acquaintances often like to give advice. They think they are being helpful, but their comments can be hurtful. "Just relax," is something people often suggest. "Why don't you go on vacation to take your mind off things?" is another. The implication is that if couples just stopped thinking about it so much, they'd surely get pregnant. Such advice can make intended parents feel like it is their fault they haven't had success.

Researchers have not been able to determine conclusively if and how stress impacts fertility, but we do know that going through infertility can be quite stressful. Listening with compassion, without judging or making suggestions, may help intended parents feel more supported.

With extra support from their family, friends, and colleagues, Steve and Stephanie were ready to learn more about IVF. Their doctor answered all their questions. They met with a nurse who told them about the timeline, the fertility medication, the office visits, and the surgery. They knew what to expect and were ready to take on IVF.

Stephanie ordered the supplies. They arrived in a gigantic box. She unpacked it and set everything out on the coffee table. It was an enormous amount of medicine vials, disinfecting wipes, syringes, and needles. Stephanie and Steve read and reread the complicated, detailed instructions. They hoped that if they measured precisely and followed the steps exactly, they'd see a baby at the end of this long, expensive road.

The first step in Stephanie's IVF journey was to shut down her body's ovulation-menstruation cycle. This allows the fertility team to precisely track egg development and schedule egg retrieval at the ideal time. She began with three weeks of birth control pills and about a week of hormone injections. After this suppression period, Stephanie began taking additional hormone shots to ramp up egg production—hopefully resulting in ten to fifteen mature eggs.

Steve was in charge of the injections. As a public safety officer, Steve was certified as an emergency medical technician and well trained in administering shots. Steve would swab the injection site on Stephanie's belly with rubbing alcohol to sterilize the skin, carefully measure the medicine into a syringe, gently jab Stephanie with the needle, and press the plunger to inject the hormones. Injections had to be done twice a day. Stephanie was working full-time, and Steve worked twenty-four-hour shifts. Sometimes Stephanie had to go to the fire station for her medication. Coordinating these meetups could be challenging, but being in charge of the medication enabled Steve to be part of the process.

While shots in the soft fat of the tummy are less painful than shots in the muscles of the arm, Stephanie's abdomen was sore and splotched with black-and-blue bruises. Some days she got headaches. But for her, the most annoying side effect from the hormones was pain in her joints—her ankles, knees, hips, fingers, wrists, and jaw all ached. To help keep Stephanie's spirits up, they invented a chocolate reward system. Every time Stephanie got a needle jab, she also received a Junior Mint!

> Every time Stephanie got a needle jab, she also received a Junior Mint!

Stephanie returned to her clinic every few days. At each visit, the doctor drew her blood to check her hormone levels and did an ultrasound to check her ovaries. He also looked to see how many eggs were developing and if they were developing at the same rate. The goal was to have many eggs all around the same size. When needed, Stephanie's doctor adjusted her fertility medication to slow down or speed up egg production.

After about two weeks of stimulation medication, Stephanie had lots of big, similar-sized eggs sitting in her ovaries. It was time for a trigger shot—a fatter needle injected into the muscle of the buttocks. The medication causes the ovaries to finish maturing the eggs and prepare for ovulation. But before Stephanie ovulated, she went into her fertility clinic to have the eggs surgically removed.

In the operating room, a doctor gave Stephanie anesthesia so she wouldn't feel any pain. Then Stephanie's fertility doctor used an ultrasound machine to guide a long, thin needle through her vagina and into her ovaries. He carefully suctioned the eggs into a test tube. He passed the test tube to the embryologist, who positioned seven mature eggs onto a petri dish and then placed the dish into a warm incubator so the eggs could rest. The incubator was the same temperature as Stephanie's uterus. The entire process took about thirty minutes.

While Stephanie was having her eggs removed, Steve was producing a sperm sample. The embryologist took the container with Steve's semen and prepared the sperm for fertilization. For people using frozen sperm, this is when the sperm is thawed.

Later that afternoon, it was time to join the egg and sperm cells. Using a high-powered microscope and a very thin needle, the embryologist plucked up one of Steve's sperm and injected it directly into one of Stephanie's eggs. The embryologist repeated the process for all the remaining eggs. Afterward, the embryologist put the petri dish back into the incubator.

The next day, Stephanie began taking different medication, this time to help her uterus develop a thick, soft lining. The injections had to go into her muscle, so it was a bigger needle, like the trigger shot. But Steve was on it, and he only had to jab Stephanie once a day.

The day after doing ICSI, the embryologist examined the eggs under the microscope. All seven eggs had successfully fertilized! Over the next two days, the embryologist kept a close eye on the embryos inside the incubator as they began to divide into more cells. During this observation period, one of the embryos stopped growing. Stephanie's sister tried to comfort Stephanie by telling her that it was only a couple of cells. To Stephanie and Steve, they had lost something a lot more meaningful than some random cells. But they were grateful that they had six embryos that were continuing to develop.

After embryos develop in a petri dish for a few days, one or more are transferred into the uterus. Sometimes an embryo is placed in the uterus three days after fertilization. The theory is that the embryo will do better developing in a uterus than in a petri dish. Other times an embryo is transferred to the uterus on the fifth or sixth day after fertilization, when it is more advanced. Waiting a few extra days can give the embryologist more time to determine which embryos look the most robust.

To help decide when to do the transfer, an embryologist grades the embryos. They look to see if the cells are dividing and if all the new cells are around the same size. The embryologist also checks that the cells are not fragmenting, or breaking into pieces. Then they grade them—A, B, or C. An embryo with a high grade is more likely to lead to a successful pregnancy and develop into a healthy baby. Stephanie remembers thinking it was like seeing "Grade A Eggs" marked on an egg carton at the grocery store!

Three days after fertilization, not all of Steve and Stephanie's embryos were grade A, but plenty of them were. The doctor recommended they transfer two embryos to Stephanie's uterus.

Before the embryo transfer, Stephanie was instructed to drink a lot of water because having a full bladder helps the fertility doctor get a good view of the uterus. The fertility doctor threaded a catheter through her vagina, past her cervix, and into her uterus and deposited the two embryos. The whole process took about fifteen minutes. The embryo transfer was not painful, but it was uncomfortable because Stephanie really had to pee. Finally, after the transfer, she was allowed to go to the bathroom!

The embryologist froze the four remaining embryos. When they are frozen, the embryo's cells do not continue to divide and develop.

Stephanie and Steve had to wait about two weeks for a pregnancy test to show an accurate result. The period between the embryo transfer and the pregnancy test is often called the dreaded two-week wait. They tried to stay busy with work, friends, and family, but it was hard to think about anything else. To them, those two weeks felt like an eternity. Stephanie wanted to stay positive and calm, but she was nervous. She tried not to get her hopes up too much—just in case IVF hadn't worked.

Finally, the big day arrived. Stephanie headed to her doctor's office for a pregnancy test. With IVF, the doctor does a blood pregnancy test to get an exact measurement of the hCG level in the patient's blood. After she had her blood drawn, Stephanie went into work. Coworkers knew that Stephanie and Steve had done IVF and that this was the day they'd know whether their efforts had paid off. She told her coworkers the game plan: when she received the call from the doctor's office, she was going to grab her purse and leave. She explained to them, "It might be the best news of my life, and I want to share it with my husband first, or I might be a wreck and come apart. So when I get the call, I am going to keep a poker face and step outside."

She turned to her whiteboard where she kept a tally of how many needle jabs she had gotten during her IVF journey. Every time she got a blood test, she added a tally. Every time she got an injection of medication, she added another tally. The jab for the pregnancy test that morning was needle number seventy-three.

Finally, the fertility clinic called. Stephanie showed no emotions, grabbed her purse, and drove to Steve's work. By the time Steve came outside to where she was waiting in the parking lot, Stephanie was sobbing. But Steve also saw her huge smile. He knew it was good news. Three days later, Stephanie returned to the fertility clinic to verify the results of the first pregnancy test. When she got to work later that

MULTIPLES, PART II

Having more than one egg in the fallopian tubes or placing more than one embryo in the uterus after IVF increases the chances of having twins, triplets, or more. Multiples are much more common than before due to fertility treatment. But having multiples can be risky, health-wise, for the pregnant person and the developing fetuses. As IVF has become more successful, transferring just one embryo has become the standard of care.

morning, she added a second pregnancy test needle jab to her tally. The total was now seventy-four.

Later that day, when she got the call from her fertility clinic, it was more good news. Stephanie was really and truly pregnant. Her uterus was able to maintain the pregnancy all on its own. No more hormone shots!

When Steve and Stephanie went in for their first ultrasound, they were surprised to see not one but two implanted embryos. They were each about the size of a grain of rice. They were having twins!

Everything still looked great a few weeks later at their second ultrasound. Stephanie said goodbye to the staff at the fertility clinic and began seeing a regular obstetrician-gynecologist, or OB/GYN for short.

During pregnancy, Stephanie had expected to be miserable. That's what so many people told her would happen with multiples. But she wasn't. To Stephanie, pregnancy was a joy. She welcomed all the typical aches and pains, even the nausea and swollen ankles. They reminded her that she was finally pregnant.

At thirty-eight weeks, it was time to nudge the twins out into the world. Stephanie's OB/GYN induced labor. Twenty-six hours later, Stephanie's cervix was fully dilated and her doctor instructed her to start pushing. With each contraction, Stephanie took a deep breath and bore down. She did this over and over again for two and a half hours, but the babies refused to come out. As Stephanie likes to say, "Once we had those two embryos in my body, they did not let go." Stephanie ended up needing a C-section.

The twins, Lily and Rob, joined their older siblings, Nate (twenty-one), Lizzie (nineteen), and Haley (eleven). When Lily and Rob were born, they also became an aunt and an uncle because a year earlier, when Stephanie and Steve were struggling to get pregnant, Nate and his wife had a baby girl.

Jason, Megan, and Caroline

Steve and Stephanie's story doesn't end here. Before intended parents even begin IVF, they have to decide what to do if they have extra embryos— embryos they no longer need because their family is complete. Some people discard them according to strict medical protocols. Other people donate remaining embryos to science so that researchers can study diseases and develop new treatments. Embryonic cells have been used in hundreds of thousands of research projects worldwide so that scientists can better understand injuries and illnesses and develop medicines and vaccines. People may grant permission for clinics to use them to test new IVF techniques or to train embryologists. Some people give their remaining embryos to another family. The other family uses the donated embryos to grow their own family. This is called embryo donation, or embryo adoption. Others keep remaining embryos frozen, though this is expensive. Some people are so conflicted about what to do with frozen embryos that they stop paying the storage fees and leave it up to the clinic or laboratory to decide how to handle them.

What people decide to do often depends on their views about the embryos. Some people think of embryos the same way they think about egg and sperm cells. Other people consider embryos to be more than a

EMBRYO DONATION

Intended parents find embryo donors in a number of ways. They may know someone who went through IVF and has extra embryos to share. They can connect with embryo donors online, through websites and apps. Fertility clinics and agencies also help intended parents connect with embryo donors. They are similar to sperm and egg banks in that they store frozen embryos and help families sort through profiles to select the embryos that are a good fit for their family.

cluster of cells. They believe that an embryo is a child waiting to be born. Others land somewhere in between.

Stephanie and Steve believe that human life begins at fertilization. Before they went ahead with IVF, they agreed that any embryos they created would have to be transferred to a uterus to give those lives a chance. Therefore, they decided that if they had remaining embryos after doing IVF, they would give them to another infertile couple. Since infertility was such a long, heartbreaking experience for them, they really wanted to help another family.

After the twins were born, Steve and Stephanie started the paperwork to donate their four remaining frozen embryos to another family. They created a donor profile, complete with their medical information, their family health history, photos, and lots of other personal information. The idea was to provide enough details that intended parents could select embryos that they felt were a good fit for their family. Stephanie and Steve also had to decide whether they wanted the donation to be known, unknown, or identity release.

Stephanie and Steve decided to do a known donation. They planned to offer their names and contact information to the recipient family. But they did not require the same amount of openness in return. As Steve explains, "Being a parent is so hard, we did not want them to feel like someone was looking over their shoulder, judging them." So Steve and Stephanie decided that they would leave the type of communication and amount of contact up to the recipient couple.

When the twins were about ten months old, the embryo donation center matched Steve and Stephanie with Jason and Megan. The couples reviewed each other's profiles. Jason and Megan had written a "Dear Donor" letter to prospective donors, telling them about themselves and why they wanted to build their family through embryo adoption. Everyone felt that it was a great fit, and they decided to move forward.

Steve and Stephanie signed a legal agreement giving Jason and Megan custody and control of the four embryos and any resulting children. In the agreement, Steve and Stephanie were granted the right to know when Megan and Jason did the embryo transfer, if it resulted in the birth of a baby, the sex of the baby, and the baby's first name. Jason and Megan also agreed to send them a photo of the newborn. Other than that, it was up to Megan and Jason to decide what, if any, additional information they wanted to share.

With a legal agreement in place, Megan and Jason moved ahead with the embryo transfer to Megan's uterus. It took two tries, using two embryos each time. The second attempt resulted in the birth of a little girl, Caroline. Jason and Megan sent Stephanie and Steve a birth announcement with a photo.

Until then, communication between the two families went through a social worker at the embryo donation center. When Steve and Stephanie responded to the birth announcement, they shared their full names, phone numbers, and email addresses. Stephanie and Steve were thrilled when Megan and Jason shared their contact information too. At first, the families communicated through email and texts, sharing news and photos. Updates gave everyone in both families great joy.

Since then, the two families have met in person a couple of times. Stephanie and Steve describe Megan and Jason as "kind, compassionate, optimistic, intelligent—everything we hope to be!" They add, "We're honored to be part of their story, even if it did include seventy-four needles."

Caroline is now four years old. Lily and Rob are six. The twins have some picture books that explain IVF and embryo adoption. Steve and Stephanie want them to know their story, but for now, they have little interest in it. When they are a bit older, Steve and Stephanie hope they will better understand IVF and better grasp their connection to Caroline. For now, they refer to her as their "special friend." Jason and Megan also plan to tell Caroline about her genetic relationship to the twins. In the meantime, both couples appreciate IVF as the gift that kept on giving.

Mikhail, Adar, Zoe, and Zachariah

When Mikhail met Adar at a beach party, he told him all about his life. He shared his likes and dislikes, his joys and sorrows, and all the experiences that had shaped him. His parents had divorced when he was young, and they now lived all over the world, from the Middle East to Europe. They have always known that Mikhail is gay and accept him fully and completely.

Adar had never met anyone as open and honest as Mikhail. Feeling brave, Adar told Mikhail all about himself. He grew up in a very religious family and conservative community. Adar's dad, who is Muslim, made it clear to Adar that being gay was a sin. So, although Adar's dad knew that his son was gay, they never talked about it. Adar couldn't share his feelings or ask his parents any questions about having crushes or dating. Despite this, Adar was very comfortable with his sexuality and unapologetic about who he was.

As a kid, when adults asked Adar what he wanted to be when he grew up, he didn't respond that he wanted to be a firefighter or an astronaut, as kids typically do. He told them he wanted to be a dad. This always gave his mom a good laugh, and his friends made fun of him. They reminded him that he was smart enough to do anything he wanted. In Adar's eyes, though, being a dad was the highest possible achievement.

That night at the beach party, Adar told Mikhail his dream. He wanted a partner, kids, a house, a backyard, and dogs. Adar wanted to be as normal and accepted by society as any straight person.

Very soon after their first date, Adar and Mikhail fell in love.

About two years later, they were ready to make Adar's dream of becoming a dad come true. Although they had many supportive friends, they knew that not everyone in their community was accepting of LGBTQIA+ people, let alone gay couples who wanted to have kids. Mikhail and Adar feared that if they had a family, their children would be teased and stigmatized. They decided to pick up their lives and move to Canada, where nontraditional families were more welcome.

> In Adar's eyes, though, being a dad was the highest possible achievement.

After they settled into their new home and jobs, Adar began researching all the possible ways they could form a family. He gathered information from friends, blogs, and online communities. He learned about egg donation and gestational surrogacy. Adar liked the idea of having a "mini me"—a small version of himself! But egg donation and gestational surrogacy cost thousands and thousands of dollars, and he knew it would take them many years to save that much money. They were ready for a family now.

A couple of times, women they knew offered to be their gestational surrogate, but for one reason or another, they changed their minds. Without a friend or family member who was willing to be a surrogate for very little money, they couldn't afford that route to parenthood.

Next, they looked into adoption. But it was just as expensive as egg donation and surrogacy. Plus, some adoption agencies in Canada refuse to work with single parents or people in same-sex relationships. Even if they could find an agency to work with, some birth mothers will only relinquish their children to straight, married couples. It could take a long time for a birth mother to choose them. When they looked into adopting a child from outside of Canada, they discovered that many countries ban adoption for LGBTQIA+ parents. Adoption within Canada or abroad were both dead ends.

Although Adar and Mikhail were disheartened, they did not give up. Adar continued to research, ask questions, and learn from other people's experiences. One day he chatted with a surrogate online who told him about an organization that gives grants to individual men and gay partners to help them build their families. Adar and Mikhail decided to give it a try. They filled out a lengthy application, wrote essays, submitted their financial statements, handed over their medical records, and completed an interview. While they waited to hear if they would be awarded money, something unexpected changed their lives forever.

Adar got a call from his brother, Zane, who still lived in the small conservative town where they had grown up. Zane told Adar that his girlfriend, Alima, who he had only been with for a short while, was pregnant. But due to health problems and financial constraints, they were unable to raise a child. Adar immediately told Zane and Alima that if the pregnancy posed no health risk to Alima and she was willing to continue carrying the child, he would adopt the baby. Alima knew Adar from their youth and trusted that he would be a great parent. But still, was this what she wanted? Alima and Zane took several weeks to think about it. Eventually, though half-heartedly, they decided to place the baby with Adar.

Toward the end of her pregnancy, Alima and Simone, Adar's mom, flew to Canada to live with Mikhail and Adar. Alima was very honest with everyone. She said she didn't know how she would feel once the baby was born or whether she would be able to relinquish the child to Mikhail and Adar. But she also said that the only reason she had continued the pregnancy was because they had agreed to adopt the baby.

ROADS TO FAMILY

MONEY MATTERS

Some ways of bringing children into a family can be practically free. But building a family can be very expensive. In addition to medical expenses, there are often fees for lawyers, psychologists, social or caseworkers, travel, maternity clothes, and more. Almost always, intended parents pay all the bills. Some people have high-paying jobs or health insurance that covers some or most of the medical aspects of human reproduction. Others have to take out loans, borrow money from friends or family, apply for grants, or make other tough financial decisions. Here are some of the costs for intended parents to build their families:

- Insemination in a health clinic, $250 to $4,000
- IVF, $15,000 to $20,000
- Hiring an egg donor or purchasing eggs from a cryobank, $25,000 to $75,000 ($5,000 to $25,000 goes to the egg donor)
- Purchasing sperm from a cryobank, $300 to $1,000 per vial ($100 to $1,000 goes to the sperm donor)
- Hiring a gestational surrogate through an agency, $150,000 to $220,000 ($35,000 to $75,000 goes to the surrogate)
- Hiring a genetic surrogate through an agency, $110,000 to $160,000 ($35,000 to $75,000 goes to the surrogate)
- Using donor embryos, $10,000
- Fees for storing frozen eggs, sperm, or embryos, $500 per year
- Infant domestic adoption, $20,000 to $45,000
- International adoption, $25,000 to $70,000
- Fostering and adoption from foster care, $0

Raising children is also expensive. According to the US Department of Agriculture, an average middle-class family will spend about $13,000 a year on child-related expenses. Factoring in inflation, that's a total of about $285,000 by the time the child turns eighteen. Housing accounts for 29 percent of expenses, 18 percent goes to food, and 16 percent goes to cover expenses related to childcare and education.

Though Alima was conflicted throughout the pregnancy, she often felt that the baby belonged to Adar and Mikhail and that she was carrying the baby for them. Adar felt the same way. While Alima was pregnant, he developed a deep connection with the baby. In addition, since Adar and Zane were brothers, Adar and the baby would have a close genetic connection. Adar was excited that he might get a little "mini me" after all.

When it was time for Alima to give birth, Mikhail drove her and Adar to the hospital and then went home to get Simone. When the nurse at the check-in desk looked up and saw Alima and Adar, she assumed they were husband and wife. As a result, Adar was able to be in the delivery room with Alima. Mikhail and Simone had to wait on the edges of their seats in the waiting room. When Zoe was born, it was a momentous occasion for all of them.

For a few months, Alima continued to live with Adar and Mikhail to help take care of Zoe. Though it was a difficult decision, Alima did decide to permanently place Zoe with Mikhail and Adar. They met with a lawyer, Alima relinquished her parenting rights to Adar, and Adar gained full custody of Zoe. When couples are married, both parents can usually adopt a child from a birth parent at the same time. Since Adar and Mikhail were not married, they would have had to complete an additional process called second parent adoption to declare Mikhail as Zoe's other legal parent. Rather than go through more adoption steps, their lawyer recommended that they simply designate Mikhail as Zoe's legal guardian. If anything happened to Adar, Mikhail would legally be able to raise Zoe.

The day Alima boarded the airplane home is still a painful memory for all of them. But they were confident that they had made the right decision for Zoe's well-being.

Just as the dads were settling into life with their daughter, they got another life-changing phone call. The grant they had applied for to grow their family through egg donation and surrogacy had come through. Adar and Mikhail knew they wanted more children. But they struggled with the idea that their children would have two completely different birth stories. The dads did not doubt their ability to love their children equally, regardless of genetic connections. But how would the children feel? Would one feel like they belonged in the family more than the other? The dads knew that they couldn't answer these questions. They just had to have faith that when their children knew and understood their conception stories, they would know they were equally loved and wanted. They accepted the grant.

Adar and Mikhail researched and selected an egg donation and surrogacy agency and began learning about what lay ahead: There'd be tons of paperwork, medical exams with a whole team of doctors and nurses, a mental health screening with a counselor, legal consultations with an attorney, and meetings with insurance agents and financial advisers to help sort out all the expenses. Even though they had a grant, they would still be responsible for some of the cost.

After completing the initial paperwork, Adar and Mikhail chose a fertility clinic and went in for medical exams, blood work, and semen analyses. The doctor deemed both men fit and their sperm healthy.

The next step was sorting through the egg agency's database to select an egg donor. At home, Adar and Mikhail projected the egg agency's website on their giant TV screen. With a group of their closest friends, they read through the profiles.

First they looked for someone who was identity release. If their child ever had questions about the donor or their genetic history, they wanted to be able to get answers. Adar and Mikhail also looked for someone with their same racial and ethnic identities and who shared their physical characteristics, so that their child would look similar to them. They also wanted someone who was smart, shared their interests, and they could relate to. They made a selection and notified the donor agency. Adar and Mikhail signed a legal agreement establishing that eggs removed from the donor's ovaries would belong to them and that they would be responsible for any children born from the donor's eggs.

EGG DONORS

People find egg donors much the same way they find sperm donors. They can ask someone they know, like a family member, friend, colleague, or acquaintance. Websites, social media, and apps also help intended parents connect with egg donors. Some fertility clinics have egg donor programs. Sometimes they recruit donors. Other times, one patient can save on the cost of their fertility services if they share some of their eggs with another patient.

Egg banks are another option for intended parents. Egg banks are just like sperm banks. They recruit donors and store cryopreserved eggs. An intended parent can look through egg donor profiles and select a donor who is a good fit for them. The donor's frozen eggs are then shipped to the intended parent's fertility clinic.

Intended parents can also use egg agencies. They operate a little differently than egg banks. Intended parents sort through donor profiles and pick a donor they like. But an egg agency does not store and ship frozen eggs. A donor has their eggs extracted at the intended parent's fertility clinic only after they've been selected.

Just like sperm donors, egg donors can be known, unknown, or identity release. Egg donors also sign legal agreements with egg banks, egg agencies, or intended parents.

With the legal documents signed, the egg donor could begin taking medication. First she took hormones to shut down her ovaries. Then she began taking fertility medication that caused her ovaries to develop lots of same-sized eggs. After a couple of weeks of egg production, the egg donor took a trigger shot. Thirty-six hours later, the fertility doctor surgically removed the mature eggs from her ovaries. The egg donor's job was done!

An embryologist fertilized half of the donor's eggs with Mikhail's sperm and half with Adar's sperm. After developing in the petri dish for five days, they had thirteen embryos.

Then it was time for the embryos' first exam. When an embryo is about five days old, it usually has more than one hundred cells. At this point, an embryologist can safely remove five to ten of those cells without damaging the embryo. The removed cells are sent to a laboratory for genetic testing for potential problems with their genetic material. Some people choose to have genetic testing done on their embryos, and others do not.

Immediately after removing the cells, the embryologist freezes the embryos to pause their development. When the genetic test results come back, the doctor uses the information along with the embryo's grade to determine which embryo to transfer to the uterus. Placing a hearty, robust embryo increases the chances that it will implant and develop into a healthy fetus.

The genetic test results were not what Mikhail and Adar were hoping for. Of the thirteen embryos they started with, eleven embryos were unlikely to lead to a successful pregnancy. Only two embryos were genetically healthy. One embryo was formed with Mikhail's sperm and the other from Adar's.

Before deciding which embryo to use, Mikhail and Adar needed to select a gestational surrogate. The same agency that helped Adar and Mikhail find an egg donor also helped them find a gestational surrogate. The agency sent Adar and Mikhail a handful of surrogate profiles. The dads looked at photos, read descriptions of the surrogate's age, sexual orientation, race, ethnicity, and religion; learned about their academic degrees and professional experience; and found out about their hobbies and what they liked to do for fun. They also saw whether the surrogate was married, how many kids they had, and why they wanted to be a surrogate.

At the same time that Mikhail and Adar were looking through surrogate profiles, gestational surrogates were reviewing their profile, which contained much of the same information. When Adar and Mikhail matched with a gestational surrogate, the agency set up a phone call so

GESTATIONAL SURROGATES

People find gestational surrogates similarly to how they might find a genetic surrogate. Sometimes family members, friends, neighbors, or colleagues offer. Other people connect online. Others work with a surrogacy agency, which helps intended parents match with a surrogate and guides everyone through the steps of the surrogacy journey.

The application process for a gestational surrogate is similar to that of a genetic surrogate. However, gestational surrogates can be older than genetic surrogates since their eggs are not used to create the embryo.

they could get to know one another and answer questions. After talking, they all agreed to work together. But there was a catch: The surrogate first wanted to complete her university studies. Adar and Mikhail agreed to wait for her. But a year later, when she earned her degree, she changed her mind. She no longer wanted to be a surrogate. Adar and Mikhail were extremely disappointed.

Once again, the agency sent Mikhail and Adar gestational surrogate profiles and shared their profile with new surrogates. As one of the surrogates, Maggie, flipped through a bunch of formal, stiff-looking photos of intended parents, she didn't see anyone she connected with. Then she came across a photo of a total goofball. His hair was disheveled, and he was making funny faces. She laughed out loud and knew that Adar was her guy. Adar and Mikhail felt the same way about Maggie. Her profile really resonated with them. Plus, she and Mikhail had the same initials, which felt like a good sign. When Mikhail and Adar talked to Maggie on the phone, they knew it was the right fit. Maggie went to Adar and Mikhail's fertility clinic. She had a full medical exam, including blood work and an ultrasound of her uterus. She also had a psychological evaluation. Maggie was in excellent physical and mental health.

Then Maggie, Adar, and Mikhail met with a counselor separately and together. They talked about their hopes for their relationship before, during, and after the birth of the child, and how they would handle things if those expectations weren't met. They also had to sort out and agree on what they would do if things went wrong. Sometimes the surrogate has a miscarriage. Other times, unhealthy pregnancies have to be terminated with an elective abortion. The counselor talked to everyone about the circumstances in which they would agree to end a pregnancy. Would they end a pregnancy if Maggie's life was in danger? Would they end the pregnancy if they thought the baby would be born with a very serious medical condition? All the adults involved with surrogacy have to agree on what to do in these situations before they can move forward. The counselor also helped everyone identify family or friends who would provide emotional support through the ups and downs of the surrogacy journey.

Next, Maggie, Mikhail, and Adar signed a surrogacy agreement. In it, Maggie agreed to give up her parental rights to any child she gave birth to. Mikhail and Adar agreed to take full responsibility for the child. Although surrogacy laws vary from country to country and state to state, Adar and Mikhail lived in a province that allows all couples to become a baby's legal parents as soon as a baby is born.

With the medical testing, psychological screening, and legal paperwork completed, Maggie could start preparing her uterus for an embryo transfer. She began taking hormonal medication to halt ovulation and menstruation and so her uterus would develop a thick, nutrient-rich lining. A fertility clinic near her home monitored Maggie and provided updates to Adar and Mikhail's clinic. After about three weeks, Maggie's uterus looked ready for a pregnancy. Maggie drove to Adar and Mikhail's fertility clinic for the embryo transfer.

But which embryo to choose? The doctor encouraged Mikhail and Adar to pick the healthiest embryo, regardless of whose sperm was used to produce it. This turned out to be the embryo fertilized with Adar's

THE PROBLEM WITH BIRTH CERTIFICATES

In the US, a birth certificate typically reflects parentage—who a child's legal parents are—but they do not by themselves establish legal parentage. The laws establishing parentage vary from state to state and may depend on a number of factors, such as who is married to whom, who gave birth, and who is genetically related to a child. When a child is adopted, their original birth certificate is sealed and an amended birth certificate is issued with the name(s) of their adoptive parent(s) but only after a court process is completed. For those who are born via known donor conception or surrogacy, establishing parentage can involve complex paperwork, adoption procedures, and/or other court processes. Same-sex couples must often jump through additional legal hoops to ensure their parentage is established and recognized throughout the country. Some people feel that a birth certificate should record someone's complete conception, birth, and parenting history. Other people believe that this information should be captured on a different document. What do you think?

sperm. About two weeks after the embryo transfer, Maggie shared that she was pregnant!

Almost every day throughout the pregnancy, the dads talked, texted, or video chatted with Maggie. They also accompanied her to important medical appointments. Maggie had been a gestational surrogate before. That surrogacy didn't result in the birth of a child, but she was very knowledgeable about the whole process. Plus, she had kids of her own. She loved being pregnant and was an expert in handling all the challenges of pregnancy, such as morning sickness, backaches, swollen ankles, and not being able to tie her own shoelaces. Adar and Mikhail trusted Maggie to keep the baby healthy and safe.

At the end of the pregnancy, Maggie had some medical complications. The doctors scheduled an emergency C-section. Adar, Mikhail, and Zoe jumped into the car and rushed to the hospital, but they missed

Zachariah's birth by five minutes. Even though they couldn't be there for the birth of their son, Mikhail and Adar were grateful that Zachariah and Maggie had come out of the experience healthy and well.

Thanks to birth parents, an egg donor, and a gestational surrogate, the two dads have two children, each with their own unique combination of genetics. Mikhail's family knows Zoe's and Zachariah's birth stories, and they love the children equally and unconditionally. Who they are genetically linked to does not affect how they feel about the children. Adar's parents avoid talking about the children's origins because they go against their beliefs on how children should be conceived. Over the years, however, they have come to see that what really matters is not how the children became part of the family but how much joy they bring to everyone. They love the children wholeheartedly. Though Adar's parents still don't openly acknowledge Adar and Mikhail's relationship, they have come to love and accept Mikhail as their own son.

Mikhail and Adar think about connectedness a lot. Although having a "mini me" felt important to Adar at one time, the couple understands that genetics alone are not what forms strong bonds or makes a family. They feel that love is actually what unites a family. They have lots of examples of this. Mikhail does not feel like less of a dad to his children than Adar, although Mikhail does not share DNA with them. Zoe loves Alima, whom she calls Mommy, and adores Zane, whom she calls Uncle. Zachariah is genetically related to his egg donor, whom he has never met. He does not share genetics with Maggie, but he has a close relationship with her. The dads know that only time will tell how important genetic ties will be to their children. They also know that their children's feelings about it will likely change over time.

As the kids get older, they have started asking about the similarities and differences between a birth mother and a gestational surrogate. The dads have books and dolls to try to help them explain. Adar and Mikhail know their kids will one day ask how babies are made, and when that happens, the dads will add those details. They admit that figuring out the best way to explain it to their kids sometimes feels like a huge task. The dads want to tell them the truth, but they also want to protect their kids from possibly feeling weird or different. They also have to navigate the religious and cultural beliefs on Adar's side of the family. Ultimately, they want both of their kids to grow up proud of who they are and how they came to be part of their family.

The dads also have a secret plan brewing that they hope will shake up the genetic mix in their family even more. They still have one frozen embryo made with the donor's egg and Mikhail's sperm. If they transfer the embryo to a gestational surrogate and she gives birth, the child will share DNA with Mikhail and the egg donor. They think that this would help each kid in their family see that genetics are important to who they are but that DNA is not what brings them together as a family.

For Mikhail and Adar, family began with love and a strong desire to have children. They hope their kids grow up in a world that accepts that families come together in different ways. As Adar explains, "No matter how you create your family, you are as normal as your neighbor."

An Egg Donor's Perspective

Lilah has been an egg donor seven times in three years. Lilah laughs, "Who knew that so many people would want a Chinese-Jewish egg donor?"

Lilah's egg donor adventures began with an application to an egg donor agency. She reported a ton of information about herself, including her race, ethnicity, religion, sexual orientation, family health history, educational level, professional experience, and interests. She was interviewed about her motivation for being an egg donor and submitted photos of herself as a child and as an adult, as well as pictures of her own kids. With Lilah's detailed information, the egg agency put together an egg donor profile and posted it on their website.

Lilah was open, honest, and thoughtful in her responses because she knew that these details were important to intended parents. Lilah knew that the more she revealed about herself, the easier it would be for intended parents to figure out if she was the right egg donor for them.

Each time a family selected Lilah, she went through the same steps. She'd have a medical exam to show that her body was healthy, a mental health evaluation to prove that she knew what was being asked of her, and a consultation with a lawyer to sign agreements. She'd then take fertility medication and, after a few weeks, have her eggs extracted.

Lilah's first two donations were split cycles. This is when two families share the cost of an egg donor and divide the eggs. Because these cycles were anonymous, she does not know if her donations resulted in the birth of any children.

Not knowing anything about the outcomes of her first two donations made Lilah uncomfortable. So she switched to an egg donor agency that valued more openness. For all future donations, although Lilah would still be anonymous, she would be told a little about the families that were receiving her eggs, how many eggs fertilized, how many embryos formed, how many children were born and their sex, and what happened to any additional embryos (for example, if they were destroyed or given to another family). Lilah was elated when her third donation ended in the birth of a little girl, and the couple sent her a photo through the egg agency.

Next, Lilah donated twice for the same couple—they wanted enough eggs to create siblings. After a few emails through the egg agency, Lilah and the recipient couple decided to ditch their anonymity and share their personal contact information. Lilah loves being able to have a personal relationship with the couple and is looking forward to when her eggs are successful in helping them grow their family.

Lilah does not yet know the outcomes of her sixth or seventh donations, but she'll be updated as things unfold. If any babies are born, she will receive birth announcements and annual updates.

Lilah suspects that most parents who tell their children of their conception will refer to her as their egg donor, egg mother, or bio mom. Lilah calls her donor offspring egg children. But she does not think of them as her children in any way, nor does she think of them as family. To Lilah, her husband and three children are her family. She imagines that if she ever met her donor offspring, she might feel some sort of connection—but not as though they were her own kids.

It's important to Lilah that donor-conceived people have access to their genetic identity. Lilah knows that she has no control over whether parents tell their children that they are egg donor-conceived, but over the years she has learned from donor-conceived people just how hurtful withholding the truth can be. She explains, "I don't think it's fair not to tell a child. What if the child wants to know about their genetic history? . . . Who am I to deprive them of that?"

Lilah has told the egg agencies she's worked with that she is available to answer any questions from past recipient parents or their kids. She has also registered with online donor databases and completed genetic tests through AncestryDNA and 23andMe. Lilah will not actively look for recipient families or offspring, but if they complete a genetic test or log onto any of the registries, they will be able to contact her. She has done what she can to make herself available to anyone looking for her.

"I am so happy I donated. I definitely have no regrets," Lilah says. "At the end of the day, I am really grateful that I was able to help so many people grow their families."

A Gestational Surrogate's Perspective

Emily gave birth to her daughter, Alexis, as a result of donor insemination. Emily's amazing experience with assisted reproduction inspired her to become a gestational carrier. That way she could be pregnant (which she loved) and help other LGBTQIA+ people create families.

Since Emily didn't know anyone looking for a gestational surrogate, she joined a website designed to help surrogates and intended parents find one another. She wrote a short blurb about herself, her family, her career, and why she wanted to be a gestational carrier. Her hope was to find someone she connected with. She wasn't looking for a best friend or to have day-to-day involvement in anyone's life, but she wanted it to feel like more than a business transaction. Emily knew that gestational surrogacy would connect the two families for the rest of their lives, and she hoped that she and the intended parents would become friends.

Through the website, she discovered a lesbian couple, Nancy and Hillary. Emily and her wife, Elaine, got to know Hillary and Nancy through emails, phone calls, and video chats. Emily also learned why Hillary and Nancy needed a gestational carrier. They had successfully created embryos with their eggs and a friend's sperm, but they both had a medical condition that prevented them from safely carrying a pregnancy.

After about two weeks of communicating back and forth, they all felt as though they were a great fit for one another. They chose not to work with a surrogacy agency. Instead, they decided to do an independent surrogacy. Emily, Nancy, and Hillary liked the idea of working directly with one another to coordinate all the surrogacy activities themselves.

Though they did everything perfectly, Emily's first try at surrogacy ended with a negative pregnancy test and great disappointment. But Hillary and Nancy wanted to try again, and they were able to do so a few months later. This time, nine months after the embryo transfer, Emily gave birth to Charles. Emily recovered from her scheduled C-section in one room, and Nancy and Hillary got their own hospital room, right next door. Emily pumped breast milk for Hillary and Nancy to feed to Charles with a bottle. Extended family popped in and out of both rooms. They talked, laughed, and took turns holding baby Charles.

The two families remain close. They FaceTime, exchange holiday cards and birthday gifts, and have visited each other several times. Alexis (eleven) and Charles (nine) do not see each other as siblings—their relationship is more like that of cousins.

Emily felt so successful as a surrogate that toward the end of her pregnancy, Emily began her own gestational carrier agency. Over the next seven years, she helped hundreds of intended parents and carriers with their surrogacy process.

Emily has been asked a lot of questions about surrogacy. One that comes up repeatedly is, How can you give up your baby? Emily knows that when people ask this, they don't usually intend to be insensitive, hurtful, or judgmental. Often they are just curious. So whenever Emily answers, she always tries to do it in a way that's educational.

To help paint a clear picture, Emily invites people to imagine themselves babysitting their friend's kids or a niece or a nephew. "At the end of the night, when it's time for you to leave the child with their parents, will you have a really difficult time leaving? Will you be really sad or depressed? Or will you more likely say, 'That was really fun. I'll see you next time!' " She continues, "You care about the kids you are babysitting, you want them to be safe and to have a good time with you. But it's not the same as when you take care of your own kids. You are not attached to them in the same way. That's what surrogacy is like. It is a completely different mindset from having your own child."

CHAPTER 4

Beyond Assisted Reproduction

WE'VE TAKEN A CLOSE LOOK AT THE VARIOUS WAYS

people make babies. But sex, insemination, and IVF are just some routes people take to grow their families. In this chapter, we want to explore two additional ways that adults bring children of all ages into their lives: fostering and adoption. Intended parents may choose to foster or adopt for moral, legal, or health reasons. For example, someone who is unable to carry a pregnancy may choose to adopt. A couple may foster to support people in their community. Adoption and fostering come with their own unique benefits and challenges, just as sex and assisted reproduction do.

ALL KINDS OF FAMILIES

There are more types of families than can possibly be captured in this book. Below are a few other common family terms.

- **BLENDED OR BONUS:** when a parent/parents have children from a previous relationship
- **CHILDFREE:** adults living together in a loving relationship without kids, either by choice or circumstance
- **CHOSEN:** where individuals choose to support one another regardless of genetics or marriage
- **CO-PARENTING:** when individuals who are not in a sexual or romantic relationship raise a child or children together
- **EXTENDED:** when relatives, such as grandparents, aunts, uncles, and cousins, live together

It's also important to note that families are dynamic—they tend to change over time. Families change for many reasons, such as marriage, divorce, death, incarceration, immigration, and the need to take care of elderly parents. One family may, over the course of many years, include elements of some or all of the family types listed above.

Adoption

Adoption is a process where parental rights are transferred from birth parents to adoptive parents. Intended parents may choose to adopt a child in their own country, called a domestic adoption, or pursue an international adoption. Kinship adoption is when a child is adopted by a relative such as a grandparent, aunt, or uncle, or someone they have a close relationship with, such as a teacher, coach, or a good friend of the family. Transracial adoption is when a child is a different race or ethnicity than the adoptive parent(s). Adoption can take place immediately after a child's birth, but it can happen at any age, including as an adult. Adult adoptions are often done to establish a legal relationship, such as when a stepparent adopts a stepchild.

Adoptions can be open or closed. In a closed adoption, no identifying information is shared between the birth and adoptive parents. After the adoption is finalized, the child's original birth records are sealed. In some states, these records become available to the child when they turn eighteen. In other cases, adoptees may never be able to access their birth information.

Most adoptions in the US are now open. The amount of openness can vary greatly from family to family. Birth and adoptive families might share yearly updates through the adoption agency or stay connected through social media, phone calls, texts, or video chats. Sometimes birth and adoptive families spend time with each other. Some develop a close relationship. Research shows that openness benefits everyone—especially adoptees, who may feel lost or confused about their identities. Open adoption gives adoptees the choice to stay connected with their birth families; the opportunity to know their racial, ethnic, and cultural identities; and the ability to access their family medical history.

But relationships between birth and adoptive families are not always possible, which can be emotionally difficult for birth parents, adoptive parents, and adoptees to navigate. For some adoptees, the experience of being separated from their birth families is traumatic. Trauma-informed adoption can empower adoptive parents to meet their child's needs.

Fostering

Foster care is a temporary living arrangement for children whose parents are in crisis and cannot care for them. Typically, children are placed in foster care due to unsafe living conditions or because of abuse or neglect. Children stay elsewhere while their parents receive the support

ADOPTION BY THE NUMBERS

In 2019 about 115,000 children were adopted in the US. Of those, about 66,000 children were adopted from the US foster care system, and about 50,000 were adopted through private adoption agencies or with the help of an adoption lawyer. About half of the 50,000 private adoptions were stepparent adoptions. In addition, about 3,000 children were adopted from other countries. The largest numbers came from China (819), Ukraine (298), Colombia (244), India (241), and South Korea (166).

and resources they need to establish a healthy environment. Whenever possible, siblings are placed together in the same foster home.

Being placed in foster care is a traumatic experience for most children. Foster parents work with social workers to provide a stable home environment and to maintain birth family connections for the children in their care. They bring children to health appointments, meetings with social workers, and visits with relatives when possible. Many people choose to be foster parents because they want to help families through difficult times. Some foster parents were foster kids themselves. While placements are temporary, usually lasting about a year, many foster parents form strong bonds with the children they care for.

Though the goal of foster care is to reunite children with their birth family, this happens only about half the time. Many times family reunification is not possible, and the child becomes eligible for adoption. Of the more than 400,000 children and teens in the US foster system, more than 120,000 of them are waiting to be adopted. On average kids spend about three years in foster care before being adopted. The most common kind of adoption from foster care is kinship adoption. About 9 percent of youth never get adopted and instead age out of the system once they turn eighteen.

Shawn, Jermaine, Alexander, Noelle, and Sarah

Shawn and Jermaine met online about fifteen years ago when they were in their mid-twenties. Each time they messaged back and forth, their chats got longer and longer. They kept reaching the platform's character limit, so they moved their conversation to email. When their emails got too long, they began speaking on the phone. Sometimes they'd talk late into the night and fall asleep while still on the phone. They both realized it was time to meet in person.

Jermaine asked Shawn out on a date. Shawn was really excited and confessed to a friend that she thought Jermaine might be the one that she would one day marry. But Jermaine was so nervous during dinner and the movie that he barely spoke. Shawn was bummed. She doubted that the relationship was going to work. But she decided to give Jermaine another chance, and soon thereafter, they became inseparable. About a year and a half after that first quiet, awkward date, Jermaine proposed. Six months after that, they were married.

The newlyweds were originally going to wait to start a family. But when she was a teenager, Shawn had an ovary removed. She thought getting pregnant might be challenging and suggested that starting earlier rather than later might be a good idea. Jermaine was on board.

The couple tried for a year with no luck. They went to see a doctor, who suggested some testing. Jermaine's semen analysis showed that his sperm were not likely to lead to a pregnancy. Shawn and Jermaine were devastated.

Shawn and Jermaine talked openly and honestly with each other about what they were feeling. They got their sadness, frustration, and disappointment about infertility out into the open. As Jermaine explains, "They were raw conversations, but important. We communicated respectfully and with grace." Because of their heartfelt discussions, they were able to say goodbye to the way they thought they were going to have a child together, and they made room in their minds and hearts for new possibilities.

They considered using a sperm donor. But the more they thought about it, the more they disliked the idea. They decided that they would either both be genetically related to their child or neither of them would be.

They also talked to a fertility doctor about IVF, which might work with Jermaine's sperm. But when they thought about all the doctor's appointments, medications, health risks, and expenses that IVF would require, they knew it was not the right option for them. It felt as though they'd be boarding a long, expensive roller coaster ride—a ride that, in the end, did not guarantee them a child.

What they wanted most was to be parents. With a focus on the end result—growing their family—and less on the process for getting there, they decided to pursue adoption.

What they wanted most was to be parents.

Shawn and Jermaine thought about their strengths, challenges, resources, and their hopes and desires for building their family. They were excited to adopt an infant so that they could experience parenting from as early in a child's life as possible. They also knew they wanted an open adoption from within the US so that their child would always know their birth family.

They did their research and found an adoption agency close to where they lived. They attended an orientation where they learned more about the agency, the people who would be helping them with the adoption, and the costs.

They got their finances in order. There would be lots of expenses, including the adoption agency's fees, fees to cover the birth mother's medical expenses, legal fees, parenting class fees, background check fees, and home study fees. They would also need to give the birth family a monthly stipend to help them pay for things like rent or mortgage, utilities such as phone and internet service, transportation, maternity clothing, and groceries.

Shawn and Jermaine were assigned a caseworker at the adoption agency. The caseworker gave them a long list of documents they had to gather and submit as part of their home study. The couple included their birth certificates and marriage license. They added their employment records, tax returns, and bank statements to prove that they earned enough money to raise a child. They had medical exams and submitted a doctor's report declaring that they were healthy and fit to care for a child. They were fingerprinted and attached results from a criminal background check. They submitted letters of recommendation from friends and family touting all the reasons why Jermaine and Shawn would shine as parents.

The caseworker met with Shawn and Jermaine individually and together. She asked them questions about their relationship, how they came to the decision to adopt, and what their parenting style would be like. They discussed their hopes, worries, and fears about adoption; how they handled stress; how their extended family felt about adoption; and how the adoption agency might support them before, during, and after the adoption.

Sometimes the caseworker met with them at the adoption agency. Other times, she met with them in their home. During those visits, the caseworker inspected their house to make sure it was safe and ready for a child. She checked for smoke detectors, saw that cleaning products were tucked away, and observed that window cords hung out of reach for children. If the caseworker had any concerns, she gave Shawn and Jermaine recommendations on how they could better childproof their home.

Next, Shawn and Jermaine put together a family profile. Sometimes this is a photo album, scrapbook, or a social media page. Shawn and Jermaine were asked to produce a short video. In the video, Jermaine and Shawn shared how they first met, why they were excited to grow their family through adoption, and what their expectations and dreams were for a child placed with them. They gave a tour of their house, described their daily activities, and introduced their friends. They included photos of their lives and of them engaging in their favorite hobby—dancing. After they completed all the pieces of their home study, Shawn and Jermaine were placed on the adoption agency's list of waiting families. They had nothing left to do but sit tight until a birth parent chose them.

After not too long a wait, Jermaine and Shawn got the hoped-for call from the adoption agency. A birth mom was interested in seeing their profile. She was due in three weeks! They rushed to decorate a room, buy baby clothes, and find a stroller. They didn't feel as prepared as they wanted to be, but they were ready enough. Days passed, and they didn't hear anything from the adoption agency. The birth mother's due date

BIRTH PARENTS

While adoptive parents work on home studies and take parenting classes, the adoption agency helps birth parents with all the steps to place their child for adoption. Typically, a caseworker meets with a birth parent(s) and helps them write an adoption plan. In an adoption plan, birth parents specify what they hope for in an adoptive family, what they want to happen during the delivery (for example, if they want the adoptive parents in the delivery room with them), and what they wish for in their relationship with the adoptive parents during pregnancy and after the baby is born. Some birth parents have a long list of requirements, and others form a simple adoption plan. What most birth families seek is a loving, stable home for their child. After the adoption plan is finalized, the caseworker gives the birth parent(s) a handful of profiles to review. They are profiles of families who meet the criteria of the birth parent(s) and who have been waiting the longest to adopt. After the birth parent(s) select a family they feel will give their child the kind of life they hope for them, the adoption agency notifies the waiting parent(s) that they have been chosen.

came and went. Finally, the adoption agency told Jermaine and Shawn that the birth mother had decided not to place her child for adoption.

All of that was a big wake-up call for Jermaine and Shawn. They realized that they had a lot to do before they were fully prepared for a child. Since they were fortieth on the adoption agency's list of parents waiting to adopt, they figured they had some time to get ready before they matched with another birth family. They got to work putting everything they needed in place.

The next time the adoption agency called, they were more prepared. But it still happened much sooner than they expected. Although they were far down on the adoption agency's list of waiting parents, Shawn and Jermaine were one of only two African American families waiting to adopt. Birth parents looking for a loving African American couple had chosen them. It was the clip of Jermaine and Shawn dancing that really clicked with the birth family. To them, Shawn and Jermaine were clearly a couple that loved each other and enjoyed life.

The adoption agency helped the families connect. Jermaine and Shawn met with Justine and Connor at the adoption agency. After they got to know one another, they felt like they were a great match. Both families agreed to the adoption.

They all signed preliminary paperwork. In it, Justine and Connor stated their intent to terminate their parental rights and transfer those rights to Jermaine and Shawn. Shawn and Jermaine stated their intent to take full, legal responsibility for the child. It is important to note, however, that before a baby is born, birth parents can always change their mind. In the US, even after the baby is born, birth parents usually have anywhere from a few days to a few weeks before they have to finalize their decision.

The pregnancy went smoothly. When it was time for Justine to deliver the baby, she checked into the hospital and texted Shawn and Jermaine. They arrived with plenty of time to be at Alexander's 4:05 a.m. delivery. Justine and Connor signed the final relinquishment papers right away, and Alexander was able to go home with Jermaine and Shawn.

Twice after the baby was born, Shawn and Jermaine's caseworker from the adoption agency checked in on the new family. Once she came to their home, and a few months later, they met her at the adoption agency. Each time, she asked how they were doing, answered questions, and provided them with additional information.

About six months after Alexander was born, the new family went to court to formally complete the adoption. At the hearing, a judge verified that everything was done properly and ethically. He could see that Alexander was thriving. Once the hearing was complete, Shawn and Jermaine were awarded full and permanent custody of Alexander.

The two families continue to be in each other's lives. At first, Shawn and Justine communicated through the adoption agency. Shawn would send updates and photos to the adoption agency once a year, and then the agency would pass them to Justine. But as they got to know each other, Shawn and Justine decided it would be easier to communicate directly and exchanged phone numbers. Now they are Facebook friends, and the families meet in person once a year. By having an open relationship with Shawn and Jermaine, Justine and Connor are able to see how Alexander is growing up and that he is loved, and to affirm that they made the best choice they could have made for him. It also gives them the opportunity to share their love for Alexander.

Jermaine, Shawn, and Alexander have also gotten to know Alexander's genetic siblings, Aaron and Michelle. Justine had placed her third child with Shawn and Jermaine—that's Alexander. She is parenting her second child, Aaron. Aaron and Alexander have the same birth father, Connor, so Alexander and Aaron are full genetic siblings. Justine had also placed her first child, Michelle, for adoption. Michelle and Alexander have the same birth mom, Justine, but different birth dads, so they are half-siblings. The exact genetic connections don't matter much to Alexander. As far as he's concerned, he has lots of siblings and grown-ups in his life that love him.

ROADS TO FAMILY

Shawn and Jermaine did not initially discuss the details of Alexander's adoption with their extended family. They waited until Alexander was able to understand his own origins himself. They did not want him to hear incorrect information from anyone else. Now that he is eight and knows the specifics, he gets to decide if he wants to share his story or not. And he loves sharing his story!

He sees adoption as a positive for all parties involved. "Adoption is good for those moms and dads who feel like it's too much pressure, so they can place their baby for adoption," he says. "I think that it's good for adults who get to adopt babies. Because it will make the parents very happy, and it'll make the kids feel happy too."

But this family story doesn't end here. About two years after Alexander's adoption, Shawn and Jermaine were ready to grow their family. But this time, they decided on a different kind of adoption. While listening to the radio, Shawn learned about embryo adoption. She did some research and talked to Jermaine. They both really liked the idea of adopting embryos from a family who had extras after doing IVF. This time, not only would they expand their family, but Shawn would also get to experience pregnancy and childbirth.

Jermaine and Shawn found an embryo donation agency they liked and followed many of the same steps they took to adopt Alexander. They had to submit lots of paperwork: their marriage license, birth certificates, health records, financial accounts, and letters of recommendation. They had to have another criminal background check and home inspection. They took classes. They wrote a "Dear Donor" letter to families donating their embryos, describing themselves, their family and community, and what brought them to embryo adoption.

After Shawn and Jermaine completed their paperwork, Shawn underwent a medical exam to determine whether her uterus was able to carry a pregnancy. She passed her medical screening. The next step was selecting embryos.

There was a lot to think about. Jermaine and Shawn are African

American. Alexander is biracial—one of his birth parents is white and the other is Black. Shawn and Jermaine knew they wanted another biracial child so that Alexander and his siblings could connect through a shared racial identity. Shawn and Jermaine also wanted an open adoption so that their child could connect with genetic siblings and learn about their origins and ancestry. And they also wanted embryos with a high grade to increase their chances of a successful pregnancy.

With their criteria set—biracial genetic parents, open adoption, and high-quality embryos—Shawn and Jermaine were ready to look at profiles. The embryo adoption agency sent them a one-page profile of all the embryos that fit their requirements. Jermaine and Shawn sorted through them and requested more detailed profiles for the embryos they were interested in. The extended profiles contained additional medical information and a letter from the donating family. Some of them even had photos of children born from the same batch of embryos. Jermaine and Shawn could only request five extended profiles at a time. Sometimes, by the time they selected embryos to adopt, the batch of embryos had already matched with another intended family.

They found two batches of embryos that fit all their criteria. A mediator from the agency (similar to a caseworker at an adoption agency) connected Shawn and Jermaine with each of the donor families so they could ask and answer questions and get to know one another. Both families agreed to place their embryos with Jermaine and Shawn. One family would be their primary donor, and the other would be their backup. Backup families are needed in case embryo thawing or transfer doesn't work. Rather than start the whole long embryo selection process over again, Jermaine and Shawn would already have another batch of embryos ready to go.

The mediator helped the families craft a communications agreement. In it, the families specified how often and in what ways they wanted to communicate with one another after the baby was born.

The mediator also helped the families sign legal agreements. The documents specified that the donating families relinquished their rights and that Shawn and Jermaine accepted all responsibility for the embryos and any children that resulted from their use.

With all the paperwork in place, Shawn had to prepare her body for the embryo transfer. She took medication to suppress her cycle and develop a nutrient-rich uterine lining. Every two or three days, Shawn had an appointment at a nearby fertility clinic to make sure everything was going well. Shawn's fertility clinic was in constant communication with the embryo donation agency, where the embryos were stored, and their affiliated fertility clinic. When Shawn's uterus was ready for a pregnancy, the family flew to the agency and clinic, where the medical team was preparing for the embryo transfer. The following day, the embryologist removed two donor embryos from a tank of liquid nitrogen. She thawed them, and a fertility doctor transferred them to Shawn's uterus. The process took just a few minutes. They were hopeful the transfer had been a success. But nine days later, Shawn's pregnancy test came back negative. They were crushed.

After about six months, Shawn and Jermaine were emotionally, physically, and financially ready for another try. But their backup family had decided not to donate their embryos. Shawn and Jermaine had to select a new batch of embryos, sign additional legal agreements, and craft a communications agreement with a new donor before they could try again.

They found a batch of high-quality, biracial embryos that would be a great fit for their family. Theresa, the single mom who created them, was interested in ongoing contact with the recipient family. Most important, she had successfully given birth to a child from this same batch of embryos. This meant that the remaining embryos had a good chance of working for Shawn and Jermaine.

There was one caveat. Theresa had used donor eggs and donor sperm to create the embryos. If Shawn and Jermaine were to have a child, that child would have an opportunity to meet Theresa, the embryo donor, but they would not be able to learn much about the sperm and egg donors—the people they were genetically related to. "You want to be able to provide them with all of the connections to who they are, but we don't always have that," Shawn explains. Theresa shared full profiles on both the egg and sperm donors with Jermaine and Shawn. They felt good about all the donors—egg, sperm, and embryo—and decided to move ahead. Shawn began her hormonal medication regimen again and visited her fertility clinic several times for monitoring. When her uterine lining was ready for a potential pregnancy, the whole family once again flew to the embryo donation agency and clinic.

After the procedure, the fertility doctor told Jermaine and Shawn that the transfer of the embryos went well. They were relieved. But wait. Did the doctor just say embryos? As in more than one? Yes, she did! Shawn and Jermaine had agreed to go with the doctor's recommendation on the number of embryos to place, but they didn't know what she had decided until after the transfer was done.

Nine days later, Shawn took a pregnancy test. It was positive! At her six-week checkup, the doctor did an ultrasound. She pointed to the image on the monitor. Shawn and Jermaine could see two spots the size of a grain of rice. Both embryos had implanted. They were going to have twins.

After Noelle and Sarah were born, the agency's mediator shared Jermaine and Shawn's contact information with Theresa. Sarah and Noelle have a full genetic sibling—Theresa's daughter, Amber, who was born from the same batch of embryos. Theresa also has another daughter, Nova, who is not genetically related to Amber or the twins. Both families communicate directly with each other. The parents are Facebook friends and have exchanged emails.

According to Alexander, he has five sisters and one brother: Noelle and Sarah, Amber, Nova, Michelle, and Aaron. As Alexander explains, "Thankfully my other sisters don't live with me . . . because that'd be a little too much."

Shawn thinks that kids at school might be a little confused about the number of Alexander's siblings, but she knows that Alexander isn't confused at all. Jermaine and Shawn have been open and honest with him from the beginning. From his own birth story, Alexander was

ROADS TO FAMILY

already familiar with the concept of biological parents. Alexander was six when he got to see his dad giving his mom her hormone shots. It was the perfect opportunity to explain to him exactly what was going on. Shawn and Jermaine told him about the embryos, and they explained how a doctor was going to put them into his mom's uterus. They kept things simple, truthful, and loving: "[Creating a baby] requires an egg from a woman and a sperm from a man. Mommy and Daddy couldn't do that, so they needed help. Sometimes the people who give the sperm and the egg are related to you and sometimes they are not." By describing the experience to Alexander, they were also practicing how they would one day tell the story to Noelle and Sarah.

Shawn and Jermaine hope that kids and families know that "family can come in all different shapes, sizes, and various methods. Each family has a beautiful story of how they came to be, a love story that blossomed with the fruit of offspring."

INFERTILITY AWARENESS

When Shawn was going through infertility, she didn't know any other African American people who were also struggling to build their families. Although infertility affects people of all races, Black women are about twice as likely to deal with infertility as white women. While on bed rest in the hospital during the last month of her pregnancy, Shawn shared her story with lots of people. They, in turn, opened up to her. Shawn came to realize that many Black individuals and couples were suffering through infertility alone. As Shawn explains, "Infertility is something that just isn't talked about in the African American community." Shawn and Jermaine hope that by sharing their story, they can help educate and support other families who have to sort through a lot of tough choices on their own journeys to parenthood.

CHAPTER 5

Donor-Conceived Perspectives

RYLIE IS A TALENTED, ACCOMPLISHED ROWER. WHERE does Rylie's athleticism come from? Did she become a strong rower because her family was big on sports and she was able to learn to row at a young age? Did she inherit that trait from her mom, who is also super athletic? Or did it come from the sperm donor her mom used to conceive her? For people like Rylie, conceived with sperm from an unknown donor, it can be hard to figure out what's nature versus nurture. In other words, it's difficult to know what's been passed down from whom and what has developed as a result of their experiences or their environment.

Donor-conceived people who are interested in figuring out which of their characteristics, skills, and personality traits come from their unknown sperm or egg donor tap into a variety of resources to find clues. Registries, DNA tests, and genealogy records can provide answers; the internet and social media can deliver leads; and connecting with donor-siblings can fill in some gaps. Sometimes people figure out who their previously unknown donor is and learn about their genetic links straight from the source.

Kianni, Rylie, Sheena, and Espy are donor-siblings. They grew up in different families, but about twenty-five years ago they were all conceived with sperm from the same unknown donor, Donor #2757. This chapter shares their insights, attitudes, struggles, and joys around being donor-conceived and explores how their experiences shaped them and their understanding of family. Though their perspectives are about their own experiences with sperm donor conception, they regularly echo the perspectives of those born through egg and embryo donation.

Kianni

Kianni's mom, Ruth, knew from an early age that she wanted to become a mother one day. So when she turned nineteen, Ruth and her partner at the time, Jenny, went to see a fertility doctor. As Ruth explained to four-year-old Kianni, "The doctor showed me a bunch of different seeds. I picked out a very special one and the doctor planted it in Mommy's tummy. That grew into a baby."

As Kianni got older, her mom elaborated that "the special seed that created you came from a man—an actual person with a name." Her mom answered her questions and showed her the man's profile from the cryobank. The donor was unknown, so the profile was the only information Ruth had to share. Donor #2757 was tall, with wavy brown hair and hazel eyes. His profile said he was German, Irish, and Native American. He was smart, loved to surf, and was into photography. Kianni used the information from the donor's profile to paint a picture in her head of who her biological father was.

Rylie

When Rylie's moms, Nicole and Lauren, were ready to grow their family, they also chose Donor #2757. He seemed smart, athletic, creative, and kind, and his physical characteristics matched Nicole's. Since Nicole would be carrying the pregnancy, they wanted the baby to look like her. When children and parents look alike, strangers are less likely to ask nosy, intrusive questions. Rylie, like Kianni, grew up knowing her conception story. Rylie has fond memories of Nicole reading a picture book to her about a kid with two mommies. When Rylie was six, her moms split up. A few years later, Nicole met Sarah, who had three children from a previous relationship. Rylie grew up in a blended family with her mom, stepmom, and three stepsiblings.

Espy

Espy's parents, Debra and Kris, fell in love in their early twenties. When they were ready to have a baby together, they agreed on insemination using an anonymous sperm donor from a cryobank. Since Debra was going to be pregnant and give birth, they decided to pick Donor #2757 because he had creative traits similar to Kris's. With an egg from Debra and sperm from a "quirky artist," the intended parents hoped that their child would be a combination of both of them.

Kris was assigned female at birth and identified as a butch lesbian as a young adult. Kris uses the term *butch* to describe a woman who looks masculine or dresses in a masculine way. By the time Espy was two, Kris identified as male. Kris began taking hormones so that his body would more accurately reflect his gender. Over the course of a few months, the testosterone caused his period to stop, voice to deepen, and facial hair to thicken. The fat around his hips and thighs shrank, and the muscles in his arms and legs became more defined. Kris also had surgery to remove his breasts. After transitioning, instead of having Espy call him Dad, Kris chose the name Beda. Beda stands for "butch dad." It's a name that honors both his maleness and his history as a butch lesbian.

When Espy was about five, her parents decided to grow their family. They had wanted to adopt a baby from Kazakhstan, but it wasn't possible. Many countries, including Kazakhstan, do not allow LGBTQIA+ parents to adopt. So they decided on insemination, with sperm from the same donor they used to conceive Espy—Donor #2757. Soon after, Debra gave birth to Espy's brother, Asa.

SEX AND GENDER

Many people think that sex and gender are the same thing, but they aren't. Usually, when a baby is born, a doctor, midwife, or parent looks at the newborn's genitals to determine if the baby is female or male. But it can be more complicated than that. Sex is determined by our biology: our anatomy (our internal and external reproductive body parts), our hormones, and our chromosomes.

The term intersex refers to people whose bodies (reproductive anatomy, chromosomes, and/or hormones) do not fit neatly into the binary concepts of female or male. Some intersex traits are obvious at birth, some are not discovered until puberty or later in life, and sometimes people are never aware of them. Variations in the human body are natural and make us unique.

Gender is not related to our body. Gender is our own deeply felt inner sense of who we are, whether woman, man, somewhere in between, a mix of both, another gender altogether, or no gender.

The term *cisgender* describes people whose sex assigned at birth aligns with the gender they identify with. Some common terms people use to describe themselves when their sex assigned at birth does not align with their gender identity are *transgender*, *nonbinary*, and *gender fluid*.

Espy doesn't remember ever not knowing about her conception. "Growing up with queer parents, I knew that I had a donor from the beginning. They didn't hide that. They were very open about it."

Sheena

In the late 1990s, when Jane and Bill chose donor conception, straight couples often kept it a secret. Many men felt ashamed for having to use another man's sperm to get their wife pregnant. After an insemination at a fertility clinic, couples were told by their doctors to go home and have sex. They were encouraged to believe that the donor's sperm would simply help the husband's sperm along. They were instructed not to mention the donor insemination to anyone, not even to their children. Many people, including doctors, believed that if the truth got out, kids wouldn't bond with their father. They worried that they'd be rejected by grandparents and other relatives, teased shamelessly by their peers, and never escape feeling different. Bill and Jane followed their doctor's advice and planned never to tell their daughter, Sheena, about her origins.

When Sheena was twelve, her father suffered a major brain aneurysm, leaving him paralyzed from the neck down and unable to speak. Her mom became his caregiver, leaving her emotionally and physically drained. One day, when Sheena and her mom were in the middle of a heated discussion, her parents' well-guarded secret came tumbling out. That's when Jane told her daughter that her dad was not—genetically speaking—her dad. To Sheena, those words felt like a slap in the face. In an instant, her world was flipped upside down. "I went to my room, looked at myself in the mirror, and no longer recognized myself. I realized that half of me was unknown." Sheena was twenty years old.

"I realized that half of me was unknown."

Sheena embarked on a fact-finding mission to discover the missing pieces of her identity. The journey was difficult and painful and took several years. But through therapy and the relationships she built along the way, Sheena was able to rediscover who she was.

The Search for Donor-Siblings

At some point, it is common for a donor-conceived person (or their parent) to become curious about the possible existence of donor-siblings—people in other households conceived with egg, sperm, or embryos from the same donor. But there are many challenges in searching for donor-siblings. Information about donor-siblings isn't stored in one easily searchable database, and pulling together data from a variety of sources can be quite a task. In addition, not everyone who is donor-conceived knows it; of those that do know, not everyone wants to be discovered or contacted. Sometimes donor-conceived people or their parents are successful in figuring out how many donor-siblings there are, and even their names. Other times, they are not. Kianni, Rylie, Sheena, and Espy discovered one another in their own unique ways, yet those discoveries profoundly impacted all of them.

Kianni

When Kianni was born, Ruth registered her birth with the cryobank where she had purchased the sperm. The cryobank had built the voluntary registry mainly for marketing. They used it to advertise how successful their donors were in producing offspring. But the registry also provided a way for families that used the same donor to contact one another. When Ruth registered Kianni's birth, Kianni was the only person listed on the registry. Ruth had no idea if or when another donor-sibling would show up. Even if another family selected the same donor, there was no guarantee that they would register their child's birth.

When Kianni was about five years old, a donor-sibling finally popped up on the cryobank's registry—a brother. Kianni thought it was pretty cool to discover another person who shared half of her genetics, but because he was just a baby, she wasn't all that interested in getting to know him. It wasn't until Kianni turned thirteen that she became more intrigued by the idea of donor-siblings. After Ruth had broken up with Jenny, she had met a woman who had two sons from a previous marriage. Kianni loved her new, boisterous, blended family, so she was bummed when Ruth's relationship ended and the boys moved out with their mom. She missed having brothers around and wondered if more donor-siblings had registered with the cryobank. This time, when Ruth and Kianni logged on, they got quite a surprise. The registry showed over a dozen donor-siblings!

Ruth sent a message to one of the other moms listed on the registry. Rebecca's twin girls were just toddlers, but Rebecca had added their names in the hopes of connecting with donor-siblings. Soon the two families were emailing back and forth regularly.

Rebecca started a private Facebook group and invited Kianni, Ruth, and all the other families listed on the cryobank's registry to join. There, they shared snippets of their lives, posted photos, sent season's greetings, and wished one another happy birthday. Kianni started a spreadsheet to keep track of everyone. On the roster, she listed her donor-siblings by name, date of birth, where they lived, and when they were discovered. As families found their way to the donor-sibling group, they'd message, text, talk on the phone, and video chat. For many, what began as a genetic link grew into friendships.

Kianni and some of her donor-siblings began meeting in person. Kianni started documenting their visits on Instagram. The media soon caught wind of the story, and newspaper reporters, television hosts, and podcasters interviewed Kianni. A *Washington Post* article, "44 Siblings and Counting," was key in linking Kianni and several other donor-siblings.

ROADS TO FAMILY

Rylie

When Rylie returned home after her freshman year at college, she was ready to learn more about Donor #2757. Since he was listed as identity release and she was nineteen, Rylie had the legal right to request identifying information about him. The cryobank gave her his name, and she used it along with information from his donor profile to search for him on the internet. When she figured out who he was, she crafted an email. She didn't know exactly what to say or how to say it. While she doesn't remember her exact wording, she recalls it reading something like, "Hi. My name is Rylie, and you're my biological dad. I just wanted to say that I am so grateful for you making the decision to donate twenty years ago. I am so grateful for my life and that you made it possible. I am OK with any relationship in any capacity that you are comfortable with. I hope to hear from you."

The next day—Father's Day—the donor sent her a message back. "Hey. Nice to meet you!" The donor told Rylie a little bit about himself and suggested that Rylie get in touch with someone named Kianni. He described Kianni as "the first of the half-siblings and a ringleader of sorts."

Rylie googled Kianni's name and discovered the *Washington Post* article. Rylie thought it was wild that this person had so many donor-siblings. Then it sank in. If Kianni had forty-four donor-siblings, and she was related to Kianni, that must mean she had that many donor-siblings as well. Rylie reached out to Kianni. Sure enough, Rylie was part of this enormous donor-sibling group. Rylie's name was added to the donor-sibling spreadsheet, she joined the group's Facebook page, and she began to learn about her donor-siblings.

Sheena

Sheena's journey to the group was quite different from Rylie's. Although Sheena's mom still doesn't like talking about Sheena's conception, she did admit that Sheena was donor-conceived. Sheena hasn't been able to locate any of the paperwork from the fertility clinic or the cryobank. She does not know if her parents tossed it or if it's buried in the basement somewhere. Sheena's mom did tell her what she remembered about the donor—he was very well educated, he had studied art, and he was a writer and photographer. A scant description of the donor was not nearly enough information to help Sheena understand her missing genetic half. Where to begin?

Sheena decided to start with her ancestry. She had grown up thinking that she was English and Irish, and she wanted to know if this part of her identity was true. In the early 2000s, genetic testing became inexpensive and available to the public. For the first time, people could swab their cheek or spit in a tube, mail off their sample to companies like AncestryDNA and 23andMe, and get information back about genetic relatives and what part of the world they came from. When her genetic results came back, Sheena was relieved to discover that her ancestry was in fact what she had grown up believing it to be.

DNA tests not only give people clues about what part of the world their ancestors are from, but they can also identify genetic relatives. Sheena briefly glanced at the names, but because there were no siblings or half-siblings listed, she didn't pay much attention to this part of the report. She was just happy to have confirmed her ancestry.

Not long after getting her results back, she received a message through 23andMe from a great uncle on the donor's side. He sent her a link to the *Washington Post* article. Sheena's first reaction was that the story was interesting, but since she was an only child, she didn't really get what it had to do with her. But as she continued to read, it dawned on her, just as it had for Rylie, that she, too, was part of this enormous donor-sibling group. Over the years, as more people have taken DNA tests, additional donor-siblings have shown up on Sheena's 23andMe account.

Since 2000 additional donor-siblings have been able to find and contact one another through the Donor Sibling Registry (DSR). The DSR is an online database designed to educate, support, and connect individuals conceived through egg, sperm, and embryo donation. As of January 2024, the DSR has more than eighty-nine thousand members and has connected more than twenty-five thousand donor-conceived people with their donor-siblings or their donors. Over the years, the DSR has helped uncover and connect even more donor-siblings in Kianni, Rylie, Espy, and Sheena's group. Many of these newly discovered siblings then reach out to others through the cryobank's registry, genetic testing companies, or the groups' private Facebook page. They are also added to the sibling spreadsheet. The donor-sibling group keeps expanding as different people access the various sibling-finding tools available to them.

Espy

Espy came to the group accidentally and a bit more reluctantly. In middle school, Espy's brother got very sick. Asa had Lyme disease, an illness people can get from a tick bite. But when he first came down with symptoms, Asa's doctor couldn't figure out what was wrong. Debra worried that Asa's illness might be genetic, so she contacted the sperm bank, hoping they could give her updated medical information on the donor. Debra didn't find out anything new about the donor's health. But she did find out about the cryobank's registry—something she hadn't known about when she had purchased the sperm. Debra quickly dove in, contacted some of the families, and landed on the group's Facebook page. There she discovered that Espy and Asa were part of a large donor-sibling group.

As Debra scrolled through the Facebook feed, she announced her discoveries to Espy. "Espy, there is someone who looks like you." "Espy, there are siblings that live nearby." "Espy, they have figured out who the donor is." It all caught Espy by surprise, and she didn't know what to make of it. She shared DNA with all these people who, until then, she hadn't even known existed. Did she want to be part of a large group of strangers just because they shared DNA?

Espy was hesitant to join the group for several reasons. First, Espy already had a sibling—Asa. Did she want others? Second, it appeared that many of the donor-siblings were getting to know one another through social media, and social media wasn't Espy's thing. Third, some of the donor-siblings were quite public about being donor-conceived. They were interviewed on TV and in news articles, and they regularly posted their photos and videos on the internet. Espy was a private person, yet her

WAIT, YOU'RE DONOR-CONCEIVED TOO?

Out in the world, donor-conceived kids and teens randomly meet one another in everyday life. Though donor conception in the 1970s was mainly done through fertility clinics to help straight couples, by the 1980s cryobanks were serving the LGBTQIA+ community and shipping sperm to people's homes. For the first time, same-sex couples and single individuals could grow their families with anonymous donor conception. These parents tended to be more upfront with their kids about their origin stories. As a result, these kids were more open about it to their friends and classmates. A casual mention of donor conception at camp, at band practice, on the soccer field, and in college dorms resulted in donor-siblings discovering one another. Parents were having similar encounters. At a dinner party, one mom raised her glass to toast her donor, and another mom recognized the donor number as the same one she had used. At her toddler's music class one morning, one mom realized that another kid in the class was the spitting image of her daughter. Two moms crossed paths when they were seeking medical care for their kids who had the same rare genetic health condition. Once parents or donor-conceived individuals make a connection like this, they often tap into registries, DNA tests, and social media to continue donor-sibling searches.

personal life was getting wrapped up in these very public stories without her knowledge. Espy felt very uncomfortable and overwhelmed, and she needed space and time to decide if and how she wanted to be involved.

● ● ●

As of the writing of this book, Kianni, Sheena, Espy, and Rylie's donor-sibling group is up to seventy-five people. They have found one another through a tangled web of overlapping tools: the cryobank's registry, the DSR, genetic testing, the internet, social media, and happenstance. They range in age from five to twenty-five. So far, there are seven sets of twins and one set of triplets. The donor-siblings have single, same-sex, and heterosexual parents. The families live mostly in the US, but others are in Canada, Australia, and New Zealand. Though most are white, one family is Black, and Kianni and her mom are Hispanic. The families are of various religious, political, and socioeconomic backgrounds and live everywhere from busy cities to the rural countryside. Every time a new donor-sibling is discovered, Kianni is excited. But she also feels a little anxious about it. How many more are out there? How is she going to keep up with everyone?

First Impressions

To many donor-conceived people, finding donor-siblings is like uncovering little pieces of their own genetic puzzle. By comparing and contrasting their traits, personalities, mannerisms, skills, interests, and even medical histories, they are better able to see what about themselves likely came from the donor. They can confirm their hunches when they share bits of information they collect from the donor's profile, off the internet, and from genetic test results. Donor-siblings can also help to normalize and validate one another's experiences in being donor-conceived.

REGULATING THE DONOR INDUSTRY

Egg, sperm, and embryo cryobanks in the US are largely unregulated. The US Food and Drug Administration requires them to screen human cells for infectious diseases. But most states don't have any additional requirements. And while cryobanks are encouraged to follow best-practice guidelines, not all of them do. This hands-off approach has led to what many donor-conceived people see as unethical practices in the donor industry. Rylie, Kianni, Espy, and Sheena speak directly to sperm donation, but many of the problems they identify also apply to egg and embryo donation.

There are no limits on how often someone can donate sperm or on how many offspring can be produced using their sperm. Since no centralized database exists to track this information, donor-conceived people can never be completely sure how many genetic relatives they have. Rylie explains the potential harm that can result from this lack of transparency: "Though it would be extremely rare for a donor-conceived person to meet and date a half-sibling, it could happen. It probably has happened." For that reason, Rylie's mom always encouraged Rylie to share her conception story with her dates. If it turned out that her date was also donor-conceived, they'd have to compare notes to make sure they weren't half-siblings. Accidental incest is something that the donor-siblings and their children will likely continue to contend with for a long time.

Little regulation also means that each sperm bank decides how to select sperm donors. Some do a thorough job of checking the information a donor provides—such as their criminal record, academic test scores, and level of education. But some cryobanks do not verify donor information, including health history. They may not require genetic testing or a psychological evaluation. Some donors have lied about a significant medical problem, putting their offspring at risk for serious mental and physical health conditions. Sperm banks rarely collect updated medical information from previous donors. Often, when families report their children's genetically related health problems back to the sperm bank, the sperm bank does not discontinue selling the donor's sperm or notify other families that used the same donor.

Though anonymous sperm donation is no longer possible due to genetic testing and the internet, sperm donors can still choose this option. Many donor-conceived people understand that donors want their right to privacy, but they don't think that right is more important than another human being's right to know their genetic identity and medical history. "Donors should understand that offspring might want to meet them one day, and to be open to that," Kianni says. "If you want to be anonymous, don't be a donor. It is not fair to the kid."

Many donor-conceived people feel that money drives the sperm donor industry. Sperm banks across the world earned about $4 billion in 2018. "It's a money-hungry industry," Sheena explains. "The sperm banks know that parents will shell out a lot of money to create a family. . . . But they are not selling a brand of soda. They are making lives. It should not be driven by profit."

People are fighting for changes in the industry—and winning. In a handful of European countries, people can no longer donate anonymously. In 2022 Colorado became the first state in the US to grant donor-conceived individuals the right to know their donor's identity when they turn eighteen. The law also puts a limit on the number of families that can use a specific donor's sperm or eggs, requires cryobanks to permanently keep a donor's records, and specifies that donors must regularly update their medical information. Other states are likely to follow Colorado's lead.

While more oversight and regulation may result in greater responsibility and less fraud in the donor industry, it could also result in higher costs for intended parents looking to use these resources. Assisted reproduction is already expensive, and added costs may rule it out as an option for some families. Many activists are seeking solutions to make the donor industry more accountable and accessible.

Kianni

The first time Kianni ever met Rebecca and her twin daughters, she was both excited and nervous. Kianni remembers the day at Disney World vividly. "There was an instant connection. The girls didn't quite understand *how* I was their sister, they just knew that I *was* their sister." The girls clung to her, held her hand, and wanted to sit next to her on all the rides. It was an instant big sister, little sister relationship, and Kianni absolutely loved it. As Kianni recalls, "I didn't have to explain myself to them or tell them things about myself. I just got to be a fun big sister and enjoy my time with them."

Inspired by her role as a big sister, Kianni set a goal for herself to meet each of her donor-siblings. So far, she has met thirty. At first, it's impossible not to look for similarities and differences. As Kianni explains, "It's really cool to see how different we can all still be even though we share the same father. I can look completely different from one person, but they can look like a twin to another person. At the same time, two people that look completely different might act the same or have the same exact interests or mindset. That's really cool to discover, since we didn't grow up together."

Rylie

Rylie had a similar experience the first time she gathered with Kianni and four other donor-siblings. She immediately recognized some facial features that they shared—a similar nose and smile, a wider jaw, and a great big dimple. These shared traits enable some of the older donor-siblings to give the younger ones a glimpse of what they might look like one day. But discovering shared physical and personality traits was not the most valuable part of meeting her donor-siblings. For the first time in Rylie's life, she met others who shared the joys and hardships of growing up with two moms and of being donor-conceived. Whereas she had expected to notice everyone's genetic similarities, she hadn't anticipated just how important hearing about their lived experiences would be for her.

Sheena

When Sheena and a group of her donor-siblings got together for the first time, she too thought they looked similar, but some more than others. "I definitely got ripped off because a bunch of siblings have these adorable dimples, and I didn't get one!" Many have similar personalities and interests. Sheena and Kianni quickly discovered that they had the same sarcastic, goofy sense of humor and that they could easily bring each other to tears laughing.

But the differences have been just as important. When Sheena first realized that she was the forty-seventh donor-sibling to be discovered, she had no idea what that really meant. She remembers thinking to herself, *What does being one of forty-seven make me? Am I just a duplicate of a bunch of other people?* Seeing that the donor-siblings were unique in their own ways was comforting. Some donor-siblings are athletes, some love animals, some pursue photography, and some are drawn to academics. As Sheena explains, "Seeing the differences in the siblings eased my nerves a bit initially, because I was able to see we definitely weren't copies of each other." Connecting with, getting to know, and forming close relationships with some of her donor-siblings has been a huge part of Sheena's healing. As Sheena explains, "Something wonderful came out of the whole mess."

Espy

When Espy first looked at the photos of her donor-siblings on social media, she didn't immediately see her own face staring back at her. Except maybe the eyebrows. Since the physical similarities weren't there, she didn't feel particularly drawn to any of them. She didn't feel that DNA alone connected them in any real way.

Espy's interest in the donor-siblings didn't develop until she went off to college. There, Espy became interested in how technology impacts our understanding of family. For her senior research project, she interviewed eight of her donor-siblings. She asked them if they engage with the sibling group. If so, how? If not, why not? Through her research, Espy learned how her donor-siblings thought about family, the role of genetics, and how technology shapes their experiences and opinions. As Espy got to know some of her donor-siblings better, her connections to them felt more genuine.

● ● ●

Some donor-siblings in Kianni, Espy, Sheena, and Rylie's group have forged close connections, others relate more casually, and others remain disconnected from the group. Those relationships will likely change over time, as relationships usually do. Although connecting with every donor-sibling is likely impossible, Rylie is excited by the possibilities that such a big group brings. "Just to know that I have people everywhere I go, potentially, that I could sit down and connect with and very likely have something very much in common with, in addition to the genetic piece, is really, really cool."

The Donor-Offspring Relationship

Donor-conceived people vary greatly in their curiosity about the donor, and their curiosity often changes over time. Some have zero interest, some would just like to know what the donor looks like, some desire updated medical information, and others hope to form some sort of relationship with the donor.

Donors are about fifty-fifty in their willingness to connect with offspring that reach out to them. In some cases, donors don't want anything to do with their offspring. They may have their own families who don't know they were a donor. Some donors file court orders making it illegal for offspring to try to contact them. Other donors are willing to provide updated medical information and answer questions. Some are interested in forming personal relationships.

Kianni

When Kianni was about seventeen, Ruth and Rebecca did some internet sleuthing and figured out who Donor #2757 was. They took bits and pieces of information from his donor profile, did some online searches, and discovered his Facebook page. It wasn't hard to find him because he had made an advertising video for the cryobank. In the video, the person interviewing the donor showed him a photo of one of his offspring. It was a baby picture of Kianni! This interaction inspired him to change his designation from an anonymous donor to identity release.

Ruth messaged Donor #2757 through Facebook, and they agreed to talk on the phone. Kianni was frustrated because she was not allowed to listen in. She had to sit patiently in her room for an hour while her mom talked to her biological father. Before she'd allow any contact with her daughter, Ruth wanted to know that he was a decent person. As Kianni explains, "Even though they had a kid together he was essentially a stranger."

Kianni had to wait until she turned eighteen to meet him. He came to Orlando on a business trip, and Kianni drove to his hotel. After parking, she sat in her car for ten minutes freaking out. She was about to meet her bio dad, and she didn't know how it was supposed to go down. Should she give him a hug, shake his hand, or not touch him at all? Meeting one's genetic father for the first time was not a common experience. It's not as though she and her friends sat around sharing stories about the times *they* met their bio dad. She remembers thinking that "he is essentially a stranger, but he is also essentially my father."

"He is essentially a stranger, but he is also essentially my father."

She got over her anxiety, stepped out of the car, and went into the hotel. As she walked through the lobby, she scanned the room, looking for Donor #2757. She heard a "Hey!" and turned to see "a person who looked like someone I knew." As she walked toward him, she said, "This is so cool." He gave her a hug. He was warm and welcoming, and she immediately relaxed. She knew she was going to be able to be herself.

They spent the day together at Universal Studios getting to know each other. They went on rides and tried on goofy hats in the gift shop. The next evening, Kianni's mom joined them for dinner. Afterward, they both went with Kianni to get her first tattoo. It felt great to Kianni to "have both my parents with me" for such a momentous occasion.

Kianni broke the news to Donor #2757 about how many donor-siblings there were. He was taken aback. Until Ruth had contacted him, he hadn't thought too much about being a sperm donor. It was something he had done to earn some money back when he was in college. The sperm bank had told him that there would be a maximum of twenty kids.

Kianni learned from Donor #2757 why there were two sets of siblings—an older group and a younger one. He had donated for a couple of years when he was in his twenties. About ten years later, the cryobank asked him to donate again so that families that had children with his sperm could have genetic siblings. This made sense to him, so he came out of retirement and donated again. But instead of only offering his sperm to existing families, the sperm bank opened his profile to anyone.

Though Donor #2757 has not donated in a long time, there are still frozen samples of his sperm out there. Parents often buy a few vials of sperm at a time so that they have enough to try insemination or IVF multiple times, or so that they can have more than one kid. When parents are done growing their family, they can give leftover vials to someone else. If these remaining samples are used, there will be even more siblings.

Donor #2757 took a while to mull over what to do about the large and potentially growing number of offspring. Eventually, he decided that he was willing to answer questions but that he could not promise that he'd be willing to meet all the donor-siblings. There were just too many. Kianni understood where he was coming from. She just hoped that he didn't get overwhelmed and disconnect from the group completely.

About once a year, Kianni brings a handful of donor-siblings to meet Donor #2757. It's up to these young adults to deliver answers, stories, observations, and updates to the rest of the group.

Rylie

Rylie was nineteen when she first met Donor #2757. It was just a few months after making contact with him and learning about her donor-siblings. The visit enabled Rylie to satisfy her curiosity about him, which began when she was about thirteen. Back then, Rylie would pore over his profile and stare at the photos of him as a child and as a young man. She'd try to figure out if she looked more like him or her mom. Rylie also wondered if some of her personality came from the donor. "While my mom and I are really close, we've always operated differently in a lot of ways. She would agree her personality is more type A. She's organized and likes to be in control; I am more creative, easygoing, and adventurous."

The donor's profile had listed that he was one-sixteenth Native American Cherokee. Growing up, Rylie thought it was cool that she, too, was part Cherokee. Whenever she was asked about her race, she would proudly add this detail. As a teenager, however, she came to understand the complexity of race, ethnicity, and culture. She came to see that what is written on a piece of paper (or in a DNA test result) isn't the same as having lived life as a person of a particular race, ethnicity, or culture. Since Rylie grew up with all of the privileges of being white, she felt that it was wrong to claim an identity she didn't experience in her day-to-day life.

When Rylie met Donor #2757, she recognized that they shared many facial features—including the dimple. Though she thinks her athleticism came from her mom, she attributes her laid-back personality, her creativity, and her adventurous streak to him.

Rylie and Donor #2757 are friends on Facebook, and they chat over Messenger every now and then. It's just the right amount of contact for Rylie. Getting to know what he is all about, what he values, and

> "In my head, there had to be some villain in my story who had caused me so much pain and confusion."

what he likes to do in his spare time has helped Rylie understand herself a little bit better.

Sheena

Sheena went into her first visit with Donor #2757 not wanting to like him. "In my head, there had to be some villain in my story who had caused me so much pain and confusion." She was expecting to meet an irresponsible person who had made all these kids without care or concern for them as humans. But when she met him, Sheena realized that he was not like that at all. He hadn't known that the cryobank had lied to him about the number of possible offspring.

Sheena liked Donor #2757. He was an interesting person, they connected easily, and they had plenty to talk about. She felt that she was more like this stranger than she was like her mom, whom she had a close relationship with growing up. Sheena and Donor #2757 have a similar personality and sense of humor, and they speak with the same cadence in their voice. They also overlap professionally. Sheena is a multimedia journalist and thinks she likely inherited her interests and talents from him. Sheena could also relate to him because they were both trying to figure out the best way to navigate this new world of genetic relatives.

Turns out, he wasn't the monster she imagined him to be. It wasn't his decision to become a donor that hurt her. It was her parents' decision to withhold the truth from her that caused her pain.

Getting to know Donor #2757 has helped Sheena fill in missing pieces of her genetic puzzle and heal. "I don't necessarily conceptualize my donor as my 'dad' in the emotional sense since we only have met twice at this point, and I don't expect him to ever fill that role, nor is that what he signed up for. But meeting him and understanding his personality allowed me such an 'ah ha!' moment in understanding myself and accepting who I was a lot more."

Espy

Growing up, Espy didn't think of the donor as anything more than genetic material. She knew that her parents had chosen him largely because he was an artist, and Beda wanted to nurture this genetic trait in Espy. Espy never felt that she needed to know more about him. But toward the end of high school, Espy started wondering if she looked like the donor. The photos that her parents had from Donor #2757's profile had been lost in a move, but Espy was able to see photos and learn about him through the donor-sibling Facebook group. To her, he looked "like a funky version of Johnny Depp," and she connected with his adventurous, fun spirit. These days, she does wonder about other interests they may share and whether learning more about him would tell her more about herself.

Donor Conception in LGBTQIA+ Families

While donor conception within the LGBTQIA+ community became more popular with the rise of cryobanks, fertility clinics willing to serve them, and at-home inseminations, not everyone understood the process or was on board with the idea. Rylie, Espy, and Kianni remember some painful childhood experiences.

Rylie

When Rylie's moms were planning to have a baby, they caught a lot of flak. Many people believed that without a father, a child would grow up with emotional and behavioral problems. Research has since shown that growing up with a single parent or same-sex parents does not negatively impact the mental or physical health of children. What impacts a child's well-being, the data tells us, is not the number of parents, their gender, or their sexual orientation. What is important to a child's happiness and success is that they have at least one supportive, stable adult caring for them.

Rylie didn't think her conception story was unusual until she started school and other kids questioned her. Her classmates wanted to know where Rylie's dad was—because, they insisted, she "needed to have a dad." Rylie knew that this wasn't the case. She understood that the man who gave his part to make her was not her dad.

Although her childhood experiences no longer bother Rylie, it was really cool for her to meet her donor-siblings. For the first time, other people truly understood what she dealt with as a kid. If she had met donor-conceived people earlier, perhaps she wouldn't have felt so isolated, they could have normalized one another's experiences, and they could have helped one another respond to those annoying comments about dads.

Kianni

Kianni's experiences were similar to Rylie's. In the 1990s, having lesbian parents and being donor-conceived were not common and not considered "normal." In grade school Kianni was teased for having two moms, for being a "test tube baby," for being a science experiment, and for being a freak of nature. Kianni has heterochromia— two different colored eyes (one green and one brown). That just proved to kids that she really was a freaky science experiment. "Kids in elementary school have no filters," Kianni explains. "When they don't understand something, they can be really mean." When she was young, the teasing really upset her. But as a young adult, she is glad she isn't ordinary. "Being a freak of nature is badass."

"Being a freak of nature is badass."

Espy

Espy remembers the challenges of middle school. A few kids understood what it meant to have gay parents, but having a transgender parent was very confusing to most of her classmates. During this time, she referred to Kris as her dad. It was just easier than having to explain what Beda meant. Espy felt like she was betraying her Beda. When she went to high school, she finally felt as if she had the energy to explain her family to people.

● ● ●

Espy, Kianni, and Rylie hope that their younger donor-siblings will have more support from one another and more compassion from their peers. LGBTQIA+ families have become more widely accepted and have more legal protections. Fewer adoption agencies, cryobanks, and surrogacy agencies discriminate against LGBTQIA+ parents, and there are more resources to help people grow their families the way they want to. As the number of kids in LGBTQIA+ families grows, the more they can normalize one another's experiences with being donor-conceived.

Honesty Is the Best Policy

Parents aren't always upfront with their children about their conception stories. Sometimes it's because the parents have never come to terms with their own infertility and it's too painful to discuss. Some are embarrassed about having needed a donor. Others feel that there is still stigma and shame around donor conception. Parents think that withholding the information will prevent their children from being teased or rejected. Some worry that their children won't love them if they know the truth.

Kianni

Kianni gets lots of questions on her TikTok, Instagram, and Facebook pages from parents inspired by her story, her positivity, and her honesty.

They want to know about her experiences as a donor-conceived person, and they want her advice on how to talk to their kids about it. She always encourages families to be honest with their children from the start. "If you allow them that information, it creates a solid foundation from which they can build their self-identity and self-worth. It lets them be confident in who they are." She wants parents to know that when kids have questions about the donor, it isn't a sign that they are rejecting them. "It is OK for your kid to contact the donor and get answers to their questions. It doesn't mean that your kid wants to have or has to have a relationship with the donor. They are just curious and want the chance to ask some questions."

Kianni warns potential parents about the harm that withholding information can cause. "I think that they are going to find out whether you want them to or not. Instead of spending your life worried that your kid will find out and then hate you, just be honest with them. If you are honest with them, they are never going to hate you. You are their parents."

Rylie

Rylie refutes the argument that intended parents might be rejected by their children if they learn the truth. "You don't have to be biologically related to your child for them to see you as their parent. If you raised them, love them, care for them, are there for them, you are their parent," she affirms. "You are not going to hurt them by telling them. I don't know what it's like to have not been told, but to have been told has made it incredibly easy. It is something I have never had to come to terms with or get over. It's just been a fact of my life, like where you're from or what your name is."

Espy

Espy's parents always presented her origin story as really cool. They were never secretive or dishonest, and so Espy grew up feeling proud of how she was conceived. "I mirrored what my parents projected," she explains.

Sheena

Discovering she had been lied to her whole life harmed Sheena's relationship with her family. Sheena couldn't help wondering if her mom had lied to her about other things. "How do you watch your kid grow up for twenty years and think their donor conception is not a big deal? It is a big deal." Sheena also wonders if part of the reason she never really connected with her dad was because of the shame he felt about using donor sperm. Because of her dad's disabilities, Sheena knows she'll never know the answer to this. But it wasn't just her relationships with her parents that Sheena had to contend with. She learned that relatives had also kept her parents' secret. They betrayed her trust as well.

Now that she knows the truth, all the cover-ups seem ironic. All through her childhood, she sensed there was a big family secret. She's not sure how she knew this, but sometimes her mom would drop these dramatic statements, like "One day I will tell you everything." Sheena just never imagined the secret was about her.

Sheena understands that conversations about donor conception can be hard for parents, but she feels that keeping secrets is misguided and unethical. Sheena believes adults should disclose donor conception to their kids, and to do this as early as possible. "I wasn't told until I was an adult, and it was an incredibly difficult and painful thing to come to terms with," she says. "You can start out being really gentle in the explanation, and as time goes on introduce more complex topics."

Sheena believes that if parents tell their child their conception story honestly, their child will get it. And if the parents aren't ashamed of donor conception, their child won't be either. "Kids will understand that their dad used donor sperm because they had to use donor sperm. It wasn't because your dad didn't want you. It was because he did want you. Just because your dad doesn't share biology with you, they still love you."

Sheena doesn't think that her mom will ever apologize for withholding the truth. She still paints donor conception as necessary but not something to be proud of. She also doesn't see Sheena's donor-siblings as real family.

LEARNING ABOUT BEING DONOR-CONCEIVED

In 2020 We Are Donor Conceived compiled a survey of 481 donor-conceived people from fifteen different countries, ranging in age from thirteen to seventy-four. Only 21 percent of parents told their children they were donor-conceived as an infant or young child. A third (34 percent) of respondents learned about being donor-conceived as teens or adults. Another third (34 percent) discovered they were donor-conceived after taking a DNA test.

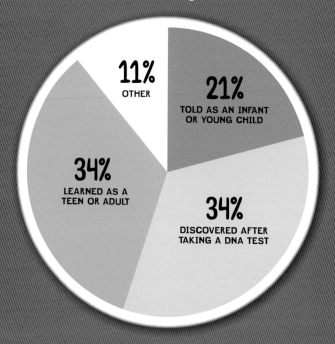

11% OTHER

21% TOLD AS AN INFANT OR YOUNG CHILD

34% LEARNED AS A TEEN OR ADULT

34% DISCOVERED AFTER TAKING A DNA TEST

"2020 We Are Donor Conceived Survey Report," We Are Donor Conceived, September 17, 2020, https://www.wearedonorconceived.com/2020-survey-top/2020-we-are-donor-conceived-survey/.

Certain factors appear to influence when parents talk to their children about donor conception. While 76 percent of children raised by single or same-sex parents learned about their origins as an infant or child, only 9 percent of children with heterosexual parents were told at a young age. As donor conception has become less stigmatized, telling children at a young age has become more common.

Sheena is not sure if her mom will ever fully see things from Sheena's perspective. But her mom is starting to acknowledge that she hurt her daughter. This has helped them regain some closeness, but they still have a way to go.

With time, the truth, therapy, and through her relationships with her donor-siblings and the donor, Sheena was eventually able to rediscover her sense of self. There are no longer any secrets, shame, or mystery hanging over her life. "My conception story, along with all my half-siblings, have become part of my identity. In a really good way." She thinks that donor conception is really cool. "It turned from a negative, traumatic thing into a really interesting, positive thing. It became something very special."

Family Ties

When defining relatedness and family, there are many perspectives. To some, family is about shared genetics. To others, it's about shared experiences: growing up together, celebrating holidays, going on vacation, visiting with relatives, and dealing with day-to-day life. To others, it's a mix of both. For Sheena, Espy, Rylie, and Kianni, what started out as a shared genetic link has grown into something much more.

Kianni hopes that all the individual relationships among the donor-siblings get them a step closer to feeling like one family. But she knows that "whether they want to meet or not depends on their personality, how they were raised, and how they feel about being donor-conceived."

Kianni

To Kianni, genetics are important. But ultimately, family is built on relationships. She and her donor-siblings have things in common because of their genetics. She considers the donor-siblings she has developed relationships with to be family. She regards those who don't want to connect or be part of the group as siblings, but not family. Kianni feels as though Donor #2757 is more of a good friend than a father. He has always been clear that he was a sperm donor and not a parent. He is willing to answer questions but not step into a parenting role. Kianni's mother adores the donor. She sometimes refers to him as her baby daddy. In this sense, Donor #2757 has become part of Kianni's family.

Rylie

Growing up, Rylie referred to Donor #2757 as her donor dad. But now she usually refers to him as the donor, or her biological father if she has to explain it further to someone. She has come to see the word *dad* as representing someone who plays an active role in raising a child.

Rylie has two sets of siblings that play an important role in her life. One set is her stepsiblings, who she grew up with. Rylie refers to her other set of siblings as donor-siblings or half-siblings—depending on the situation. If she refers to them as donor-siblings to someone, she usually needs to explain it. So, if she doesn't want to get into the whole story, she just says half-siblings. Rylie shares some unique experiences with her donor-siblings that she doesn't have with her stepsiblings. All of her donor-siblings know what it means to be donor-conceived, and many of them have grown up without a dad. Her stepsiblings came into the world in the traditional way, and have always had a mom and a dad. But overall, her relationships with her stepsiblings are much stronger than those with her donor-siblings. The four of them have played, laughed, fought, loved, and weathered the ups and downs of life together.

Rylie defines family as "where me and my mom are." But she goes further to describe her family as two overlapping circles. She places herself, her mom, and her mom's side of the family in the center. On one side is a circle of her chosen family: her stepmom, three stepsiblings, and that side of the family. On the other is her newfound donor-sibling community, which comes from her biological dad.

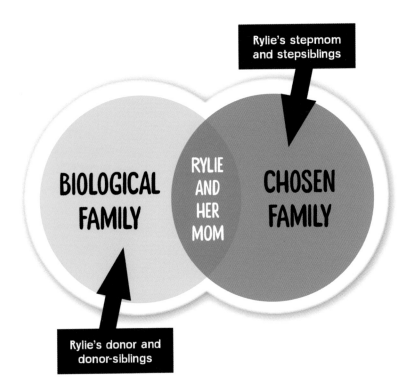

Rylie's stepmom and stepsiblings

BIOLOGICAL FAMILY

RYLIE AND HER MOM

CHOSEN FAMILY

Rylie's donor and donor-siblings

Sheena

Sheena's definition of family has expanded over the years. Her immediate family is her husband and two cats. Then she has her large family she has known since childhood—her parents, grandparents, cousins, aunts, and uncles. Sheena also has her chosen family—close friends who have been there for her more than the family she grew up with. Now she has a biological family that she didn't know about until a couple of years ago. The donor-siblings she is super close with she calls her sisters, and she describes her other donor-siblings as her half-sisters and half-brothers. She refers to the group as a whole as her half-sibling group.

Espy

For Espy, it wasn't until she interviewed her donor-siblings and wrote her senior paper that she was able to sort out her own feelings about being part of a massive donor-sibling group. She coined the term "mega family," which she defines as a sibling group with more than twenty people. To Espy, DNA does not automatically mean people are family. To her, family is more about living near one another and having shared experiences. "Family is who you choose. Family is someone you show up for. Family is someone you are available for." Espy feels as if this is impossible to do with all of her donor-siblings. How could she form relationships with people who live across the world, who are in different stages of their lives, and who haven't shared experiences with one another? Espy is trying to figure out how all these donor-siblings fit, or don't fit, into her understanding of family. She is hopeful that over time, she will form close relationships with some of her donor-siblings and that they will feel like family.

What Espy is sure about, however, is that technology plays a huge role in creating mega families. The donor-siblings are all alive because of reproductive technology—donors, insemination, and IVF. Technology also connects them. There is lots of data floating around about the donor-siblings—in DNA databases like 23andMe and AncestryDNA, on the cryobank's registry, on the DSR, on the roster Kianni keeps, in digital photographs, and on posts all over the internet. They are all connected digitally, whether they are aware of it or not, and regardless of whether they want to be part of the donor-sibling group or not.

As Espy tries to understand the role of technology in all these relationships, she thinks of one of her favorite childhood photos. In it, she is two years old. Espy and her multiracial extended family are marching in a gay pride parade. They are all wearing T-shirts that read "It takes family to raise a child." Each person is carrying a sign that defines their relationship to her, such as "Queer Aunt," "Grandpa," "Beda—Butch Dad." The picture helps Espy remember that "at the end of the day, anyone you love and helps you grow can be your family."

CONCLUSION

Family Is What You Make It

This book was all about how children come to be and how they come to be part of families. Making a human always takes the same three ingredients—an egg cell, a sperm cell, and a uterus. But just how the ingredients come together is a fascinating tale. With discoveries in science and medicine, we have insemination and IVF, along with sex, to bring babies into the world.

Sometimes the ingredients that created us come from the same people who are raising us. Other times, we don't share genetics with the people responsible for our care, such as when we are raised by stepparents, adoptive parents, or foster parents. This is also often true when donors and surrogates are involved.

Different families use different names for all the people who contribute to creating and raising children, such as *mothers, sperm donors, bio parents, gestational carriers, egg donors, birth parents, fathers, genetic surrogates, embryo donors,* and *first parents*—just to name a few! It's up to each family to decide how all the people who play a role in creating and caring for children fit together.

As a result, families come in all sorts of shapes and sizes. We have nuclear families, extended families, foster families, adoptive families, birth families, blended families, co-parenting families, genetic families, and chosen families.

So, the next time a younger kid looks up at you and asks, "Where did I come from?" you can throw your shoulders back, hold your head up high, and wow them with your explanation—one that will include them, no matter who they are or what their family looks like!

GLOSSARY

adoption: when parental rights and responsibilities are legally transferred from one parent or set of parents to another

anesthesia: medicine that puts people in a sleeplike state to prevent them from feeling pain during surgery and other medical procedures

anesthesiologist: a doctor who specializes in administering anesthesia and other pain medication to patients

assisted reproduction: medication, medical treatment, or both to help create a pregnancy

bio parent: also called a biological or genetic parent; a name that some donor-conceived people use to refer to their egg donor, sperm donor, or genetic surrogate

biological sex: the sex of an individual based on chromosomes, hormones, and internal and external reproductive anatomy

birth control: also known as contraception; a method, medicine, or device used to prevent pregnancy

birth parent: also known as a first parent; a term used by some adoptees and those raised by foster parents or guardians to refer to an adult who conceived them but who voluntarily or involuntarily relinquished their parental rights

blended family: also known as a bonus family; a family with a parent(s) who has a child or children from a previous relationship

cervix: the part of the uterus that opens to the vagina

cesarean section: also known as a C-section; a surgical procedure that entails making an incision in the abdomen and uterus to deliver a baby

chosen family: a family where individuals choose to support one another regardless of genetics or marriage

cisgender: a person whose gender identity matches the sex they were assigned at birth

closed adoption: an adoption with no contact between the birth parents and adoptive parents

coming out: when someone in the LGBTQIA+ community reveals their sexual orientation, gender identity, or both to others

conception: becoming pregnant through fertilization, implantation, or both

cryopreservation: when eggs, sperm, or embryos are frozen at a low temperature

donor: someone who provides egg cells, sperm cells, or embryos to someone else, so they can create a pregnancy. Donors can be known, unknown, or identity release.

donor-sibling: someone who is conceived with sperm, eggs, or embryos from the same donor as someone else. Donor-siblings can be half or full genetic siblings.

doula: a professional labor assistant who provides physical and emotional support to a birth parent before, during, and after childbirth

egg: also known as an egg cell or ovum; a reproductive cell often referred to as a female gamete

ejaculation: when the penis releases semen

embryo: a developing human in the first eight weeks after conception

embryologist: a scientist specially trained in creating and managing embryos in a laboratory

embryo transfer: part of in vitro fertilization (IVF), when embryos are removed from a petri dish and placed into the uterus

epididymis: a coiled tube that connects the testicles to the vas deferens. Sperm mature in the epididymis and develop the ability to swim.

extended family: relatives such as grandparents, aunts, uncles, and cousins that live together

fallopian tube: a tube that transports eggs to the uterus

fertilization: when an egg cell and sperm cell join together

fetus: a developing human from the ninth week after conception until birth

foster family: when adults are licensed, certified, or approved to care for a child or children who have been relinquished by their birth parents or guardians or removed from their birth family by the state or county government

gamete: a reproductive cell

gay: being attracted to a person of the same sex, gender, or both; often used to refer to a man who is attracted to men, but others also use this term

gender identity: a person's deeply held sense of being a man, a woman, both, neither, or another identity

genetic surrogate: also known as a traditional surrogate; an individual who is inseminated with sperm from either a donor or an intended parent and carries a fetus for an intended parent or parents

genitals: external reproductive anatomy

gestation: the period of human development from conception until birth

gestational surrogate: also known as a gestational carrier; an individual who carries a pregnancy created through IVF for an intended parent or parents

guardianship: when a child is placed with a relative or trusted adult, without the termination of the birth parents' parental rights

heterosexual: also known as straight; being attracted to a person of a different gender. Usually, this refers to men who are attracted to women and women who are attracted to men.

home study: what families go through to become eligible to adopt. A home study entails interviews, home visits, criminal background checks, health evaluations, financial assessments, and reviews of letters of recommendation.

hormone: a chemical in the body that affects the activities of cells, tissues, and organs

identity release: also known as open identity; when a donor's identifying information (such as name, last known address, email, and donation location) is released to offspring when they turn eighteen

implantation: when an embryo attaches to the uterus

insemination: when sperm is placed inside the vagina or uterus to facilitate fertilization

intended parent: an individual who hopes to become a parent using egg donation, sperm donation, embryo donation, or surrogacy

intersex: someone who does not anatomically, chromosomally, or hormonally fit the binary notions of male or female

intracervical insemination (ICI): when sperm is placed into the vagina, close to the cervix

intracytoplasmic sperm injection (ICSI): part of in vitro fertilization, when a single sperm cell is injected directly into an egg cell

intrauterine insemination (IUI): when sperm is placed into the uterus

in vitro fertilization (IVF): when egg and sperm are joined together outside of the body

kinship care: also known as relative placement; when a child or children are removed from their home and placed in the care of a relative, stepparent, or other trusted adult who has a connection with the child

lesbian: a woman who is attracted to women

LGBTQIA+: an acronym that stands for lesbian, gay, bisexual, transgender, queer/ questioning, intersex, asexual/agender, and other gender identities and sexual orientations that are not cisgender and heterosexual

open adoption: when there is some degree of communication between birth and adoptive families. It can range from annual contact through an adoption agency (or an encrypted email) to the families forming a close relationship.

ovary: one of two oval-shaped organs that produce and store egg cells

penis: an organ that transports semen and urine out of the body

private adoption: also known as independent adoption; when birth families and adoptive families work with a lawyer to complete the adoption (as opposed to working with an agency)

queer: a self-identifying term for someone who does not conform to societal expectations about sex, gender, sexual orientation, or a combination of these

relinquishment: when birth parents voluntarily or involuntarily give up their legal parental rights

reunification: when a child who was removed from their home is able to return to their birth parents or guardians

second parent adoption: when a second parent adopts a child without the first parent losing their parental rights

semen: a grayish-white liquid of mostly sperm, sugar, and proteins that is ejaculated from the penis

sex assigned at birth: the sex that a doctor, midwife, or parent assigns to a newborn baby. Sex is biological and is based on reproductive body parts, hormones, and chromosomes.

sexual orientation: romantic or sexual feelings toward other people or no people (asexual)

single parent: one parent who raises a child or children

sperm: also known as a sperm cell or spermatozoon; a reproductive cell often referred to as a male gamete

stepparent: also known as a bonus parent; a divorced adult with a child or children who marries another adult who may or may not have been married before and who may or may not have a child or children from a previous relationship

testicle: one of two oval-shaped organs that produces sperm cells

transgender (trans): someone whose gender identity does not align with their assigned sex at birth

ultrasound: an imaging technology that uses high-frequency sound waves to create an image or video of organs, tissues, or other structures inside the body, including a fetus in the uterus

uterus: also known as a womb; a muscular organ about the size and shape of an upside-down pear that contains and protects a developing fetus

vagina: a stretchy passage that leads from the uterus to an opening between the legs

SOURCE NOTES

24   "We have this . . . of it together,": George, interview with the author, May 16, 2021.

28   "Are we going . . . came to be?": George.

30   "It was a really beautiful feeling.": Elle, interview with the author, March 14, 2021.

33   "Now when people . . . think it is.": David, interview with the author, March 14, 2021.

33   "Just because we . . . be a family.": Elle, interview.

34   "We are all . . . roll with us.": Johnny, interview with the author, June 29, 2021.

34   "I come from . . . the African continent.": Johnny.

35   "Wait. Which one . . . the country, right?": Johnny.

37   "If we do this . . .": Terra, interview with the author, April 1, 2021.

38   "We were not . . . anything like that.": Terra.

40   "Wake up little . . . job to do!": Terra.

41   "Terra knocked herself up!": Laura, interview with the author, March 8, 2021.

42   "Like the appointment . . . and little fingers.": Terra, interview.

42   "I was the . . . was the oven.": Terra.

43   "We're going to . . . room right now.": Terra.

43   "Mommy, I came . . . with one hand.": James, interview with the author, March 8, 2021.

43–44   "Gosh, Mommy's tummy . . . Auntie Terra's tummy.": Laura, interview.

44   "Biology does not . . . bit of difference.": Terra, interview.

45   "I am going . . . my real mom.": James, interview.

45   "If you are . . . all of us.": Terra, interview.

51   "What? Do you . . . father to die?": Nate, quoted by Stephanie, interview with the author, May 28, 2021.

54   What's wrong with me?: Stephanie, interview.

59   "It might be . . . and step outside.": Stephanie.

61   "Once we had . . . not let go.": Stephanie.

62–63   "Being a parent . . . shoulder, judging them.": Steve, interview with the author, May 28, 2021.

63–64   "kind, compassionate, optimistic . . . include seventy-four needles.": Steve and Stephanie, interview with the author, May 28, 2021.

64   "special friend.": Steve, interview.

76   "No matter how . . . as your neighbor.": Adar, interview with the author, April 7, 2021.

76 "Who knew that . . . Chinese-Jewish egg donor?": Lilah, interview with the author, April 20, 2021.

78 "I don't think . . . them of that?": Lilah.

78 "I am so . . . grow their families.": Lilah.

80 "You care about . . . your own child.": Emily, interview with the author, June 29, 2021.

85 "They were raw . . . and with grace.": Jermaine, interview with the author, May 1, 2021.

91 "Adoption is good . . . feed happy too.": Alexander, email message to the author, July 8, 2021.

93–94 "You want to . . . always have that.": Shawn, interview with the author, May 1, 2021.

94 "Thankfully my other . . . little too much.": Alexander, email.

95 "[Creating a baby] . . . they are not.": Shawn, interview.

95 "family can come . . . fruit of offspring.": Shawn, interview.

95 "Infertility is something . . . African American community.": Jermaine, interview.

97 "The doctor showed . . . into a baby.": Ruth, quoted by Kianni, interview with the author, June 11, 2021.

97 "the special seed . . . with a name.": Ruth.

98 "quirky artist": Espy, interview with the author, April 13, 2021.

100 "Growing up with . . . open about it.": Espy.

100 "I went to . . . me was unknown.": Sheena, interview with the author, April 8, 2021.

103 "Hi.. My name . . . hear from you.": Rylie, interview with the author, March 15, 2021.

103 "Hey. Nice to . . . ringleader of sorts.": Donor #2757, quoted by Rylie, interview.

105 "Espy, there is . . . the donor is.": Debra, quoted by Espy, interview.

108 "Though it would . . . probably has happened.": Rylie, interview.

109 "Donors should understand . . . to the kid.": Kianni, interview.

109 "It's a money-hungry . . . driven by profit.": Sheena, interview.

110 "I didn't have . . . time with them.": Kianni.

110 "It's really cool . . . grow up together.": Kianni.

111 "I definitely got . . . didn't get one!": Sheena, interview.

111 What does being . . . of other people?: Sheena.

111 "Seeing the differences . . . the whole mess.": Sheena.

112 "Just to know . . . really, really cool.": Rylie, interview.

113   "Even though the . . . essentially a stranger.": Kianni, interview.

113   "he is essentially . . . essentially my father.": Kianni.

113–114   "a person who . . . is so cool.": Kianni.

114   "have both parents with me": Kianni.

115   "While my mom . . . easygoing, and adventurous.": Rylie, interview.

116   "In my head . . . pain and confusion.": Sheena, interview.

116–117   "I don't necessarily . . . a lot more.": Sheena.

117   "like a funky . . . of Johnny Depp,": Espy, interview.

118   "needed to have a dad.": Rylie, interview.

118   "Kids in elementary . . . nature is badass.": Kianni, interview.

120   "If you allow . . . ask some questions.": Kianni.

120   "I think that . . . are their parents.": Kianni.

120   "You don't have . . . your name is.": Rylie, interview.

120   "I mirrored what my parents projected.": Espy, interview.

121   "How do you . . . a big deal.": Sheena, interview.

121   "One day I . . . tell you everything.": Sheena's mother, quoted by Sheena.

121   "I wasn't told . . . more complex topics.": Sheena.

121   "Kids will understand . . . still love you.": Sheena.

123   "It turned from . . . really good way.": Sheena.

123   "whether they want . . . about being donor-conceived.": Kianni, interview.

124   "where me and my mom are.": Rylie, interview.

126   "mega family,": Espy, interview.

126   "Family is who . . . are available for.": Espy.

126   "It takes family . . . be your family.": Espy.

SELECTED BIBLIOGRAPHY

All Families Surrogacy. Accessed August 3, 2022.
https://www.allfamiliessurrogacy.com/.

The American Society for Reproductive Medicine (ASRM). Accessed August 3, 2022.
https://www.asrm.org/.

BabyCenter. Accessed August 3, 2022.
https://www.babycenter.com/.

Biro, Frank M., and Yee-Ming Chan. "Normal Puberty." UpToDate. Last modified
June 20, 2022. https://www.uptodate.com/contents/normal-puberty.

Copeland, Libby. *Lost Family*. New York: Abrams, 2020.

Donor Conception Network. Accessed August 3, 2022.
https://www.dcnetwork.org/.

The Donor Sibling Registry (DSR). Accessed August 3, 2022.
https://donorsiblingregistry.com/.

Family Equality. Accessed August 3, 2022.
https://www.familyequality.org/.

Fertility IQ. Accessed August 3, 2022.
https://www.fertilityiq.com/.

Gatlin, Marna, and Carole LieberWilkins. *Let's Talk about Egg Donation: Real Stories
from Real People*. Bloomington, IN: Archway, 2019.

Gays with Kids. Accessed August 3, 2022.
https://www.gayswithkids.com/.

Ginsburg, Elizabeth S. "Procedure for Intrauterine Insemination (IUI) Using
Processed Sperm." UpToDate. Last modified September 14, 2021. https://www
.uptodate.com/contents/procedure-for-intrauterine-insemination-iui-using-processed
-sperm?search=procedure%20for%20intrauterine%20insemination&source=search
_result&selectedTitle=1~150&usage_type=default&display_rank=1.

Ginsburg, Elizabeth S., and Serene S. Srouji. "Donor Insemination." UpToDate. Last
modified April 6, 2020. https://www.uptodate.com/contents/donor-insemination
?search=donor%20insemination&source=search_result&selectedTitle=1~16&usage
_type=default&display_rank=1.

Golombok, Susan. *We Are Family: The Modern Transformation of Parents and
Children*. New York: PublicAffairs, 2020.

Heart to Hands Surrogacy. Accessed August 3, 2022.
https://www.hearttohandssurrogacy.com/.

Hertz, Rosanna, and Margaret K. Nelson. *Random Families: Genetic Strangers, Sperm Donor Siblings, and the Creation of New Kin.* New York: Oxford University Press, 2019.

Ho, Jacqueline. "In Vitro Fertilization: Procedure." UpToDate. Last modified April 14, 2022. https://www.uptodate.com/contents/in-vitro-fertilization-procedure?search=IVF%20procedure&source=search_result&selectedTitle=1-150&usage_type=default&display_rank=1.

Human Fertilisation & Embryology Authority (HFEA). Accessed August 3, 2022. https://www.hfea.gov.uk/.

Martin, R. D. *How We Do It: The Evolution and Future of Human Reproduction.* New York: Basic Books, 2013.

Matsumoto, Alvin M., and Bradley D. Anawalt. "Male Reproductive Physiology." UpToDate. Last modified June 28, 2020. https://www.uptodate.com/contents/male-reproductive-physiology?search=male%20reproductive%20physiology&source=search_result&selectedTitle=1-12&usage_type=default&display_rank=1.

Men Having Babies. Accessed August 3, 2022. https://www.menhavingbabies.org/.

National Embryo Donation Center. Accessed August 3, 2022. https://www.embryodonation.org/.

Prager, Sarah, Elizabeth Micks, and Vanessa K. Dalton. "Pregnancy Loss (Miscarriage): Terminology, Risk Factors, and Etiology." UpToDate. Last modified June 1, 2022. https://www.uptodate.com/contents/pregnancy-loss-miscarriage-terminology-risk-factors-and-etiology?search=pregnancy%20loss%20(miscarriage)&source=search_result&selectedTitle=5-150&usage_type=default&display_rank=5.

Progress Educational Trust (PET). Accessed August 3, 2022. https://www.progress.org.uk/.

ReproductiveFacts.org. Accessed August 3, 2022. https://www.reproductivefacts.org/.

Rosen, Mitchell. "Intracytoplasmic Sperm Injection." UpToDate. Last modified March 16, 2022. https://www.uptodate.com/contents/intracytoplasmic-sperm-injection?search=intracytoplasmic%20sperm%20injection&source=search_result&selectedTitle=1-49&usage_type=default&display_rank=1.

Rupnow, Jana M. *Three Makes Baby: How to Parent Your Donor-Conceived Child.* Dallas: Rupnow & Associates, 2018.

Schattman, Glenn L., and Kangpu Xu. "Preimplantation Genetic Testing." UpToDate. Last modified April 4, 2022. https://www.uptodate.com/contents/preimplantation-genetic-testing?search=preimplantation%20genetic%20testing&source=search_result&selectedTitle=1~92&usage_type=default&display_rank=1.

Seattle Sperm Bank. Accessed August 3, 2022. https://www.seattlespermbank.com/.

Single Mothers by Choice. Accessed August 3, 2022. https://www.singlemothersbychoice.org/.

Society for Assisted Reproductive Technology (SART). Accessed August 3, 2022. https://www.sart.org/.

Surrogacy Mentor. Accessed August 3, 2022. https://www.surrogacymentor.com/.

Tinina Q Cade Foundation. Accessed August 3, 2022. https://cadefoundation.org/.

Thomson, E. "'Wait, I Have How Many Siblings?' An Exploration of the Sperm Bank Industry and What It Means to Share DNA." Undergraduate thesis, Smith College, May 7, 2021.

US Department of Health and Human Services, Children's Bureau. Accessed August 3, 2022. https://www.acf.hhs.gov/cb.

Victorian Assisted Reproductive Treatment Authority (VARTA). Accessed August 3, 2022. https://www.varta.org.au/.

We Are Egg Donors (WAED). Accessed August 3, 2022. https://www.weareeggdonors.com/.

Welt, Corrine K. "Physiology of the Normal Menstrual Cycle." UpToDate. Last modified June 1, 2022. https://www.uptodate.com/contents/physiology-of-the-normal-menstrual-cycle?search=physiology%20of%20the%20normal%20menstrual%20cycle&source=search_result&selectedTitle=1~150&usage_type=default&display_rank=1.

FURTHER INFORMATION

Books and Articles

Cha, Ariana Eunjung. "44 Siblings and Counting." *Washington Post*, September 12, 2018. https://www.washingtonpost.com/graphics/2018/health/44-donor-siblings-and-counting/.

Kramer, Wendy, and Naomi R. Cahn. *Finding Our Families: A First-of-Its-Kind Book for Donor-Conceived People and Their Families.* New York: Avery Trade, 2013.

The Learning Network. "We Are Family: 50-Plus *Times* Articles, Photos, Maps, and More about Families of All Kinds." *New York Times*, November 26, 2019. https://www.nytimes.com/2019/11/26/learning/we-are-family-50-plus-times-articles-photos-maps-and-more-about-families-of-all-kinds.html?searchResultPosition=8.

Mroz, Jacqueline. "When an Ancestry Search Reveals Fertility Fraud. *New York Times*, February 28, 2022. https://www.nytimes.com/2022/02/28/health/fertility-doctors-fraud-rochester.html?searchResultPosition=3.

Padawer, Ruth. "Sigrid Johnson Was Black. A DNA Test Said She Wasn't." *New York Times*, November 19, 2018. https://www.nytimes.com/2018/11/19/magazine/dna-test-black-family.html.

Plumhoff, Katherine. "The Egg Hunt." *Teen Vogue*, April 9, 2021. https://www.teenvogue.com/story/the-egg-hunt.

Raphael, Bette-Jane. "What Happened When I Told My Adult Daughter She Was Conceived with a Donor Egg." *Washington Post*, September 21, 2018. https://www.washingtonpost.com/news/parenting/wp/2018/09/21/what-happened-when-i-told-my-adult-daughter-she-was-conceived-with-a-donor-egg/.

Sasani, Ava. "Adoption TikTok: Building Community and Critiquing the US Adoption System." *Teen Vogue*, April 11, 2022. https://www.teenvogue.com/story/adoption-tiktok-community.

Shapiro, Dani. *Inheritance: A Memoir of Genealogy, Paternity, and Love.* New York: Knopf, 2019.

Multimedia

The Adopted Life: https://www.angelatucker.com/films

Adoptees On: https://www.adopteeson.com/episodes

Alease Daniel @aleasetheembryologist, TikTok: https://www.tiktok.com/@aleasetheembryologist

Amaze Sex Education Videos: https://amaze.org/

Biohacked: Family Secrets: https://www.biohackedpodcast.com/

Born in June Raised in April: What Adoption Can Teach the World: https://podcasts
.apple.com/us/podcast/born-in-june-raised-in-april-what-adoption-can-teach
/id1088504227

British Fertility Society: "A Guide to Fertility" Videos: https://www.britishfertility
society.org.uk/fei/videos/

Half of Us: https://podcasts.apple.com/us/podcast/half-of-us/id1453118743?fbclid
=IwAR236QN9vMgUrxRihTJ3tQ4xDPrNyevx4vBvj15JYE0-awoLGPy
DfI9zAR4&mt=2

Kianni Arroyo @donor_siblings, Instagram: https://www.instagram.com/donor_
siblings/?hl=en

"Kids Talk Vaginas with a Gynecologist": https://www.youtube.com/watch?v
=kAy5tyOz_9A

"MHB San Francisco 2019: Teen Panel: Surrogacy Children of Gay Dads Share Their
Stories!": https://www.youtube.com/watch?v=00xSZrMaFtA&t=1s

National Human Genome Research Institute: https://www.genome.gov/

Peter Mutabazi @fosterdadflipper, Instagram: https://www.instagram.com
/fosterdadflipper/?hl=en

"Radiolab Presents: *Gonads*": https://www.wnycstudios.org/podcasts/radiolab/projects
/radiolab-presents-gonads

Roads to Family: https://roadstofamily.com/

"Taken into Foster Care, through the Eyes of a Child": https://www.youtube.com
/watch?v=Gb8BGKqVVZM

"Types of Adoption as Shown by Superheroes": https://downthehobbitholeblog
.com/2020/types-of-adoption/

"(un)Wanted—Interviews with Birth Mothers and Adoptees": https://www.youtube
.com/watch?v=pVlSjBB3BmM

"Voice of Youth: Supporting Adolescents in Foster Care": https://www.youtube.com
/watch?v=vu_BAayToJA&t=1s

We Are Donor Conceived: https://www.wearedonorconceived.com

"What Adopted Children Think You Should Know": https://www.youtube.com
/watch?v=QuRPKITqmxE

You Look like Me: https://open.spotify.com/show/5vsmYdI1W2QECnKDrzTF1C
?fbclid=IwAR0QXYjUqspYIlTogb8xtMWnoMuqEL96TqnCw1vzlOHuq
TUEGS2SFAhmegg

INDEX

ACKNOWLEDGMENTS

I could not have done this without the intelligence, insights, and contributions of Jacqueline DiBernardo. She brought the concept of sperm, egg, and baby transportation systems to the work, dubbing our reproductive systems "DNA Delivery Networks."

I am eternally grateful to all the families that so generously shared their stories with me—whether their narratives made it into the book in full form or not, all of their experiences and perspectives shaped this manuscript.

Thank you to the myriad professionals who patiently answered questions, fact-checked, and lent their expertise, in particular, Paula Amato, MD, Professor of Obstetrics and Gynecology, Oregon Health & Sciences University; Astrid Castro, Founder, Adoption Mosaic; Alease Daniel Barnes, Embryologist; Carey Flamer-Powell, Founder, Surrogacy Mentor and All Families Surrogacy; John Hesla, MD, Reproductive Endocrinologist, Medical Director, Oregon Reproductive Medicine; Nash Jones, LGBTQ Responsiveness Consultant and Trainer; Senna Keesing; Kory Keller, MS, CGC, Genetic Counselor; Michelle McCann, children's book writer and editor; Amy Penkin, LCSW, Clinical Program Manager, Transgender Health Program at Oregon Health & Sciences University; Robin E. Pope, Oregon Family Formation Law Lawyer, Fellow of the Academy of Adoption & Assisted Reproduction Attorneys; Elizabeth Rusch, author and freelance editor; Ann Scott, MD, FACOG, Doctor of Obstetrics and Gynecology; and my colleagues and partners through the Oregon Youth Sexual Health Partnership.

To the amazing team at Lerner Publishing Group, past and present: Ashley Kuehl, Hallie Warshaw, Shaina Olmanson, Andrea Nelson, Danielle Carnito, and Athena Currier. I thank that talented team for wrangling my manuscript into a work of art and to those working behind the scenes to make this book a reality.

My deepest gratitude to those who provided wisdom on various iterations: Susan Alton Dailey, The Bailey-Kluender Family, Elizabeth Coleman, Shelley Darcy, Kris Francois, Susan Frisby, Kathy Jones, Kelly Luzania, Gavin and Sarah Mahaley, Carolyn Miye Sheppard, Lucca Monnie Beale, Kristen Mulvihill, Linda Pfohl, Sherron Selter, Kelly Stainback-Tracy, Susan Stanford, Patrick Symmes, Joe Taravella, Jamie Waltz, Sasha Wright, and Teri Tilley.

Thank you to my extended family, my Portland family, and my peeps from Berkeley, Happy Hour, and TKD, for your encouragement.

Finally, I could not have pulled this off without the endless support and medical expertise from my husband, Chris, and much eye-rolling from my amazing children, Hudson and Hà.

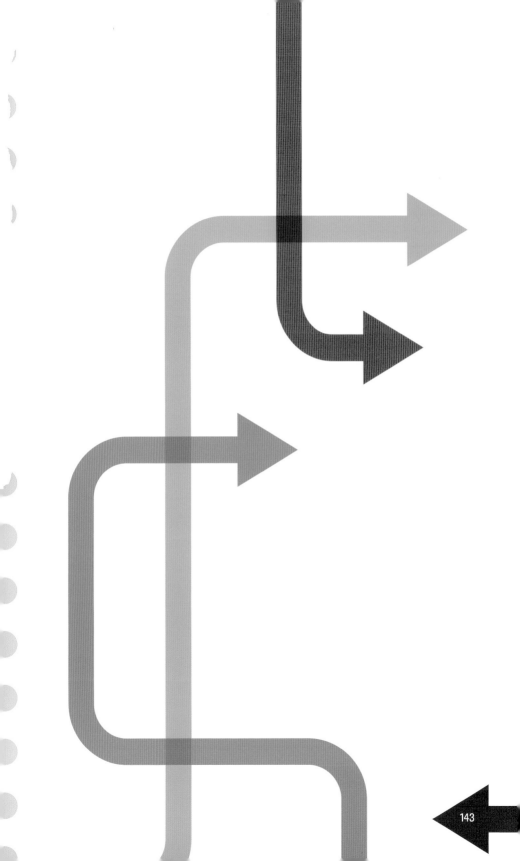

143

ABOUT THE AUTHOR

For as long as Rachel HS Ginocchio can remember, her parents answered any and all of her questions about the human body and how it all worked (sometimes they gave her more information than she actually wanted to know)! So, when other kids asked her questions, Rachel was eager to pass on her knowledge. Who knew that many years later, it would land her a master's degree in public health (MPH), a career in sexuality health education, and a passion for writing and teaching about all the ways humans reproduce and form family. Rachel lives in Portland, Oregon, with her loving husband and two spectacular children.